BUILDING
MODEL RAILWAYS

Cyril Freezer

BUILDING MODEL RAILWAYS

MODEL & ALLIED PUBLICATIONS

Model & Allied Publications
Argus Books Ltd.
P.O. Box 35,
Hemel Hempstead,
Herts,
England.

© Argus Books Ltd 1982
© Cyril Freezer 1982

First Published 1982
ISBN 0 85242 778 6

Designed by Kaye Bellman
Phototypesetting by Grange Filmsetting, Birmingham
Printed in Great Britain by Pindar Print, Scarborough

Contents

Introduction

'How do I build a model railway?. This is the most obvious, most frequent question of the beginner. He isn't helped if he listens to a group of modellers, for they are apt to contradict one another. The truth is that there are many ways, and most of them work.

Some, however, are not only more difficult than others, but call for a great deal of skill. Some are fine for quick results, but have weaknesses which show up in time.

The following methods are conventional, convenient, quick and above all tested. They are those I have either used myself, or have seen used on layouts that have stood up to a good deal of hard work. I have also kept cost clearly in mind. One or two excellent ideas do tend to require, if not a second mortgage, certainly a very large disposable income.

This book was originally issued as a special edition of 'Model Railways' in 1980. It has been revised, checked and where changes in manufacturers have occurred, amended.

C. J. Freezer

The Workshop

Whilst a model railway can be constructed with the most primitive of equipment, there is no doubt whatsoever that good, well chosen tools greatly speed the work. So for that matter, does a well organised working area.

THE KITCHEN TABLE

The traditional location for all modelling activities is the kitchen table. In the days when this was scrubbed deal and had a decent sized drawer at one end (or even a couple of drawers) this was practicable. The drawers held tools and materials, an accidental damage to the top could be removed with a judicious scrape. Modern kitchen tables aren't quite so accommodating.

The diagram shows a useful workbench/tool caddy which can sit on a melamine worktop without risk of damage to the surface, since the blockboard base rests on four rubber screw-on feet. A few

A 7ft×5ft garden shed makes a superb modeller's workshop.

This measures approximately 2ft 6in×1ft 10in and is made from 12mm ply. It has rubber feet for protecting the table-top. Plastic drawer units at the back hold tools and small parts, the power unit provides 12V dc for testing and for low voltage soldering irons, or miniature drills.

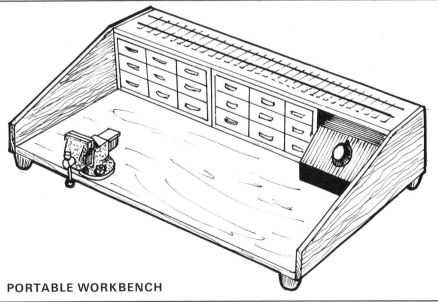

PORTABLE WORKBENCH

(Above) The author's latest modelling workbench. Plastic-faced ply has been used to provide a clean, neat finish to the vertical surfaces. The low voltage test panel has been built in at the far end. 13A switched sockets are on the front of the bench. The vice is at the RH end: this is a left-handed workbench. Small parts are in the drawer units.

(Right) Gash bag at the end of the workbench: an invaluable aid to workshop cleanliness. Once filled, it can be sealed with a wire twist and put in the dustbin.

THE PERMANENT WORKSHOP

A permanent workbench, complete with handy racks, drawers and other bits and pieces is to be preferred. Of course, space is a problem. In a permanent layout room, a workbench can usually be arranged beneath the main baseboards, assuming they are high enough, a striplight directly under the main section of layout provides ample working light.

For the more serious modelmaker, who may tend to specialise in building locomotives, coaches or wagons in preference to operating the layout, a good workshop becomes of paramount importance. The area of workbench is not so vital, most of our work can be carried out in an area as small as 2 ft × 1 ft providing there is additionally, somewhere to store the bits and pieces one needs at the next stage of the proceedings and, of course, somewhere to stand the part finished model during assembly.

A very sound scheme is to acquire a number of similar sized boxes of reasonable capacity and then arrange a tidy method of storage—a correctly sized shelf is adequate. Suitably labelled with the invaluable Dymo label maker, you can store all the necessary parts together and take them out as and when the mood

smaller drawer units for tools and components, a built-in power unit for testing, plus a length of track for testing purposes and a small vice are provided. The basis is a piece of blockboard, with a hardboard auxiliary surface over the top to take the usual wear and tear of workshop life.

takes you. In some cases a kit comes in a box which can hold the half finished model, but nowadays this is, in the main, confined to cast locomotive kits.

The workbench needs to be substantial. Probably the best top surface is the $1\frac{1}{4}$ in thick faced chipboard now used for kitchen worktops. DIY stores often offer offcuts at quite moderate prices, the melamine surface is pleasant and clean to work on, and the thickness ensures a dead working area.

A good engineer's vice is advisable, the smallest, $2\frac{1}{2}$ in pattern is adequate, the 3 in is ideal. Cheaper vices are not a good investment for the simple reason that they lose their effectiveness. A solid cast iron vice, with renewable jaws, will quite literally last a lifetime, and whilst battered, will still function perfectly.

Shelves and storage in an earlier workshop. These were behind the working area, and proved very convenient.

General view of workbench in shed. A test-track runs across the window; useful when building locos.

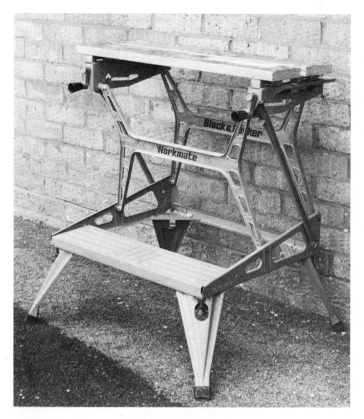

The Black & Decker 'Workmate', probably the most useful contribution to the amateur craftsman of the 1970s.

VENTILATION AND HEATING

Modelling, today, involves a wide variety of solvents and fluxes, most of which give off fumes. All fumes are more or less toxic, and whilst very low concentrations are tolerable, high concentrations can be fatal. Therefore good ventilation is essential, if there is any suspicion in your mind, install an extractor fan first and find out if it is absolutely necessary afterwards.

Whilst a workshop area needs some form of heating, it is not essential to have it anywhere near as warm as a living room. Safety is an important factor, low level electric radiants are a menace. All forms of oil heater at best put a lot of water into the atmosphere, which you don't want, and far less pleasant odours when out of order. An electric fan heater is ideal for low level use, a radiant should be mounted high on the walls.

THE HEAVY SHOP

It is very difficult to arrange a single workbench so it is suitable for fine model-making and more solid carpentry, as associated with baseboard construction. It is best to separate these two. If power woodworking tools are in use, then it is advisable to separate the functions, for it does not exactly improve modelmaking to smother everything in sawdust.

The garage is the perfect place in which to make baseboards. At one time it was necessary to incorporate a workbench, but the advent of the Black & Decker 'Workmate' has changed all this. There is no doubt at all that the 'Workmate' is one of the finest tools to come onto the market this century, for tool it is. It is also a useful trestle, a fine way of getting up to ceilings and, to show its extreme versatility, it can be used as an extremely useful perch for the operator of an exhibition layout! It is impossible to praise it too highly, one need only say that I have never met any user who was not highly enthusiastic.

It is worth pointing out that a goodly sprinkling of sawdust over the garage floor is a good thing, it soaks up any spilt oil, which can then be swept up and burned on the garden incinerator.

LIGHTING

It is vital that the workbench should be well lit and that there should be no possibility of the light shining direct into your eyes. Daylight is ideal—for part of the time. A good deal of modelling takes place in winter months and artificial light is needed. In practice, natural light is not always so convenient, for unless you can arrange a north light, or failing that, an east light (for few people model in the morning) direct sunlight can be a nuisance, not only because it makes the place uncomfortably hot, but since it tends to reflect off any bright item around, and since it moves, is always finding something fresh to catch the eye.

Whilst many people look to fluorescent light for workshop use, probably the finest light source available is a reflector spotlight which can be arranged to throw a brilliant pool of light directly where required.

Tools
For The Job

It is possible to build a complete model railway with a very small, carefully chosen tool kit, but on the other hand, the possession of a really comprehensive collection not only speeds the work, it adds considerably to the pleasure. In practice our tools fall into three loose classifications, and although there is a certain amount of overlap, the principal requirements are such that one needs, for maximum efficiency, a core of the vital tools. We shall therefore deal with each grouping separately.

BASEBOARDS

For the large timber work associated with baseboards, you require a tenon saw, a padsaw, a drill brace and a selection of drills up to $\frac{1}{4}$ in dia., a large screwdriver and a large square. The inexpensive combination pattern, which will enable you to mark off a 45° angle, is probably best. A small bradawl will have its uses, and of course, you must have a rule. A steel tape measuring in inches and mm, extending to 2 m is adequate, but the 3 m tapes are more useful all round. The combination square will have its own rule on it.

This is the basic kit. A set of chisels, or just $\frac{1}{4}$ in and $\frac{5}{8}$ in which meet most requirements. A small block plane will be needed if you intend to go in for any form of joints, whilst one of the Surform or similar rasps will also find a use.

However, the biggest step forward is

Tools are best kept safe in a small chest of drawers. This one is fixed under the workbench.

The ubiquitous
power drill.

The power jigsaw is
invaluable for
baseboard
construction.

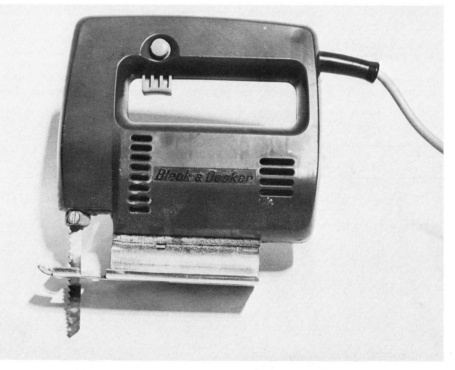

the addition of power tools. The power drill is probably the most common, since it has so many other uses, not only on the model, but around the house generally, the investment is well worthwhile. A 2-speed version is advisable, but there is little need for the more expensive hammer drill unless you have a lot of concrete lintels that need plugging. There is no need for our purpose to go for larger than a $\frac{3}{8}$ in capacity chuck.

A power jigsaw, or sabre saw, is perhaps the most useful tool for advanced railway modelling one can obtain. It is not merely that it can speed up work, it enables one to tackle certain projects such as cutting out intricate shapes in thick ply or chipboard to permit one to create

Tenon Saw.

Geared drill brace.

Below. Large
screwdrivers,
including Posidrive
and straight point.

(Bottom) Chisels,
spirit level and
pincers.

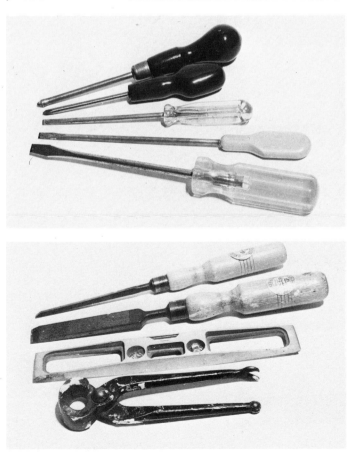

intricate multi-level baseboards with the
minimum of trouble. The latest versions,
which permit angular cuts and have provision for distance guides to enable one
to produce parallel cuts, are particularly
convenient.

GENERAL MODELMAKING

Without going into over elaborate detail,
the following tools will be needed for
general modelmaking.

    Steel rule, measuring in mm and inches
    Scale rule giving feet and inches in
    your chosen scale
    Engineer's square, 3 in or 4 in
    Dividers or compasses
    30° and 45° set squares
    Small 6 in pin ended saw
    Heavy duty trimming knife
    Fine craft knife
    Set of small drills and drill brace
    Pliers (at least two pairs, one large,
    one small, fine nose)
    Wire cutters
    Tweezers
    Soldering iron, solder and flux

This only represents the base neces-
sities and does not cover metal work.

    For this some additional equipment is
required.

    Piercing saw
    Jeweller's snips

15

Files, 6 in, various shapes, second cut or fine cut
File, 6 in flat, bastard cut
Set of needle files
Centre punch

Again this is very basic, I have not gone into taps and dies or explored the various clamps and other specialised tools employed by experienced modelmakers. Even this rather limited kit will cost a fair amount and would have to be acquired slowly.

There is a common suggestion that cheap tools are expensive in the long run. This, like many generalisations, is not altogether true. It is often a mistake to buy essential tools solely on price, but it is by no means true that inexpensive tools are necessarily of poor quality. For example, there are several reputable firms

Trimming knife: light and heavy craft knives.

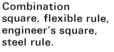

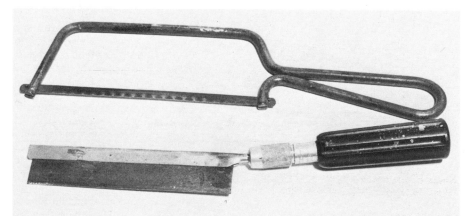

(Above right) Set of watchmaker's screwdrivers.

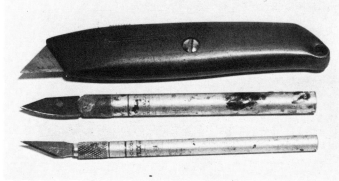

Combination square, flexible rule, engineer's square, steel rule.

Pin ended miniature hacksaw, razor saw.

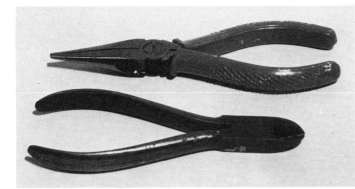

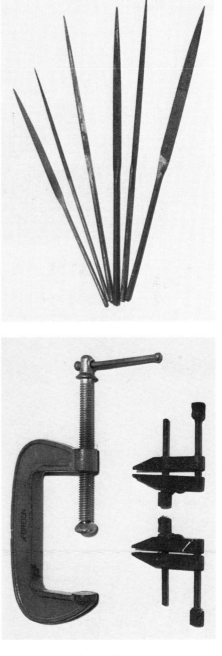

(Top left) Snipe nose pliers and wire-cutters. (Middle) Model maker's screwdrivers and tweezers. (Above) Pin punch, centre punch and scriber.

(Top right) Selection of needle files. (Below right) G clamp and pair of toolmaker's clamps.

who make a practice of acquiring job lots of sound tools and selling them at keen prices. The best place to find these firms is in the Wembley Conference Centre every January during the Model Engineer Exhibition. They are also to be found in the advertisement columns of the Model Engineer, and frequently at the better model engineering and model railway exhibitions in provincial centres. It is rather refreshing to be able to say that there are firms run by enthusiasts who consider their customers deserve good value.

There is really no limit to the number or type of tools one can find a use for in this hobby.

MACHINE TOOLS

If, in the course of time, you begin to get seriously interested in locomotive construction, then your thoughts will turn towards the acquisition of machine tools.

'Wishbone' sharpening set for small twist drills.

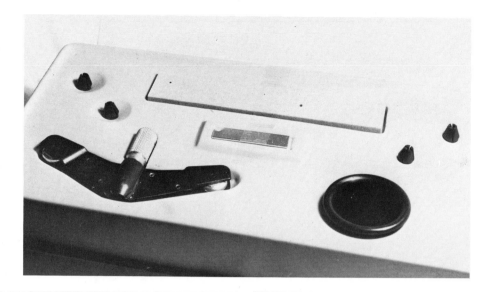

(Above) Magnifying glass on stand and vernier calipers.

(Right) Cowells precision vertical drill.

In general, the first thought is to get hold of a lathe. In point of fact, a good pillar drill is far more important; most turned parts can be bought, and a lot of the specialised ornamental turning can be carried out by the old dodge of gripping a drill horizontally in the vice and shaping the rotating workpiece with a selection of files. This was effective when we had to use a hand drill, it is even easier now that most of us have power drills.

One must also mention the miniature 12V drill, which is extremely useful when one gets down to the really small drills. It has another feature, one can get very small thin abrasive discs which will cut through small scale rails with ease. They are invaluable for putting insulation gaps in tracks that have already been laid, and greatly simplify cutting flexible track. They only look small and simple, in point of fact they need to be treated with respect; anything that can slice through hard steel can make a mess of fingers.

The lathe is regarded as the king of tools; possibly this is debatable since a computer controlled universal mill can do considerably more intricate work. However, in the home workshop, where capital expenditure has to be kept within bounds, the lathe is an extremely useful machine tool.

The best known small lathe is the Unimat, a tool which can be modified to act as a milling machine with the addition of extra parts. The Cowell 90 lathe is a slightly larger capacity conventional lathe of conservative design, which is the highest praise possible for the basic centre turning lathe, which has not materially altered in design for well over eighty years, since the pattern is regarded as incapable of improvement in any direction without impairing its utility in others. The Simat 101 is also a conventional lathe, which is supplied as a kit for home assembly.

12V drill, with wire brush and abrasive discs.

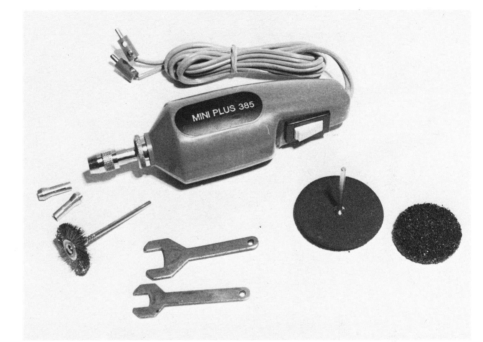

Unimat 3 lathe.

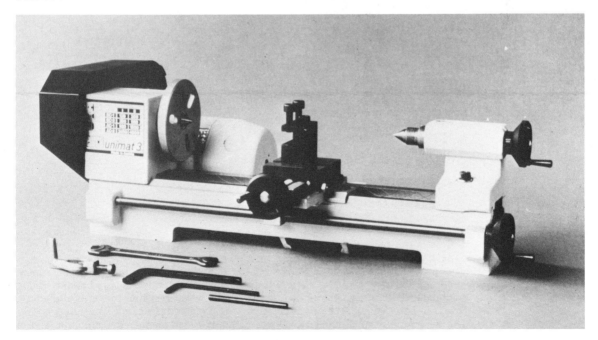

Cowells 90 lathe.

Simat 101 lathe.

This is the tally of those tools readily available at the time of writing, small enough to fit into a scale modeller's workshop. As we go to press, at least two additional imports are announced, all in the same area, about 2–2½ in centre and about 12 in between centres capacity.

SOLDERING

Once the soldering iron was an essential tool of the model railway builder. Today it only serves one essential function, electrical connections. It is needed for some forms of track construction, and in

Soldering a wire to tag strip using cored solder. In this instance, the solder is brought to the iron, so that the flux flows onto the joint.

the other area where it is still extensively employed, scratchbuilding from metal.

Furthermore, it is fairly safe to assume that most younger readers will have learned how to solder at school, one valuable change in the curriculum is the substitution of the more general subject, MI, for the old woodwork classes.

Finally, there is no longer any question of anyone using the old fashioned solid bit, heated on a gas-ring; this, more than anything else, made soldering an arcane art, solely because it took so long to learn how to judge the correct temperature. The beginner, now, uses an electric soldering iron.

There are two basic types, the standard heated element and the more recent instant heat pattern. The latter are very convenient, but fairly costly and a little more cumbersome than the type of iron best suited to our main requirement, electrical connection.

So, although a heavier duty 25 watt bit has its use in general modelmaking, the 15 watt instrument iron, with interchangeable bits, is the most suitable tool for electrical work. It is provided with a hook to enable it to be hung with the tip vertical, but ideally you should obtain one with a proper stand.

This is the most important part of the process. The second most important part is to ensure that the areas to be soldered are clean.

New solder tags, the tags on switches and the like, are normally plated or tinned so that they need no further attention.

Similarly, wire that has been freshly stripped from its insulation is clean and suitable for instant soldering. Two things will need cleaning. The first are the tags on old or surplus electrical equipment that has been stored for a considerable time in dirty or damp conditions. The second is rail.

For electrical connections, it is necessary to make a small bright patch where you want to attach the wire. For switch tags or other electrical connections, the craft knife will do very nicely. For rail, the tip of a small screwdriver will do the job.

For electrical connections you don't have to bother with flux. Simply put the freshly bared wire against the joint face—in the case of solder tags on switches, there is a hole to allow one to hook the wire in place—apply the hot bit, and touch with the end of a length of cored solder.

This should flow instantly, forming a bright bead which runs smoothly around the wire and over the tag or the rail web. That's all there is to it, except to let it cool off.

There are two possible causes of trouble. If you've not cleaned the job correctly, then the solder doesn't flow onto the part. If the iron isn't hot enough, the solder remains a grey looking putty and this dry joint, as it is known, not only fails to hold the parts securely, it also has a high electrical resistance, whereas a proper soldered joint has only an infinitesimal resistance which can, in practice, be ignored.

So much for soldering wires. For

general soldering, the essentials are, first, clean the parts, generally with fine abrasive paper. Second, apply flux. Third, tin the metal by applying the hot bit and solder.

Parts can be joined by placing the fluxed surfaces together and running the solder round the edge. Capillary action carries it through the joint.

Flux is needed to assist the solder to flow. There are pastes and liquid fluxes. The former are inactive and greasy, they are best for electrical work. For general metal work, an active liquid flux is preferable. At one time killed spirit was used, though most people relied on Bakers Fluid, which was basically zinc chloride in solution. It made a mess of most things if not cleaned off immediately.

Today phosphoric acid flux is preferred. It is obtainable as Eames 40 flux. Providing the instructions are followed, principally that the parts are washed after assembly in cold water, there should be no trouble. Phosphoric acid is also used for rustproofing, and the well known rustproofer Jenolite diluted 50% with tap water, is an excellent flux. Again, it needs to be washed off after use, it is an active flux and tends to remove the oxide film on metal.

It should be pointed out that active fluxes have the virtue of cleaning *light* oxide films off metal, and seem to have mild degreasing qualities.

It is impossible to solder oily metal, it is also, without special solders and fluxes, impossible to solder aluminium.

Baseboards

The baseboard is a functional device the sole purpose of which is to provide support for the models. It is a necessary evil, and, with the price of timber today, a fairly expensive one at that. It cannot be over-emphasised that the ultimate success of the model, in no small way, depends on the strength and solidity of the baseboard. It is not sufficient merely to be able to support, for a short while, the weight of the tracks, rolling stock and scenery, it must take the weight of the builder and, equally important, show no sign of sagging throughout its life.

TRADITIONAL FRAMING

For many years the basic framework of a model railway baseboard in Britain was a rectangular frame of 2 in × 1 in timber with cross bracing, covered with a sheet of man-made board. This particular arrangement, used sensibly, has many virtues, not the least of which being a long and fairly honourable pedigree. It is normal to keep the size of individual frames to a reasonable size—generally not exceeding 4 ft × 2 ft for private use, and to construct large layouts from a number of frames.

The concept of the individual frame is an excellent one. It enables one to carry out the initial construction work outside the railway room—possibly in the garage—and assemble the model *in situ*. Since it is possible to build each section on the workbench, with the distinct advantage that you can turn the baseboard section around, or even invert it for ease of working, construction is simplified.

It is sometimes suggested that in the event of a move, the railway can be quickly transported. Alas for this theory, Murphy's Law states clearly that on moving home, you will find that the only practical site for the layout is a totally different shape. If one is faced with the possibility of frequent moves then it is necessary to build the model a fairly loose fit on all likely sites. However, providing the baseboard sections are not too large, it is often possible to adapt the model to fit by reconstructing a couple of key sections, or even, in the odd case where the new railway room is appreciably larger, by inserting a couple of extension sections to improve the capacity of the line.

OVERALL SIZE

A size around 4 ft × 2 ft has been found convenient for ease of movement around the house. Such a baseboard can be easily lifted by one individual and carried before him vertically, avoiding damage to both the model and the decor, neither of which is exactly desirable. There are, moreover, excellent reasons for reducing the length to between 3 ft 6 in and 3 ft 0 in, for this will fit into most cars, whereas 4 ft can often be a little tricky.

There is one danger with all portable layouts, sooner or later, if the model is at all worthwhile, you will be asked to exhibit it. The advisability of this is a personal matter, it can be wearing, it will certainly test both your endurance and the soundness of your work.

It has also, over a period of years, re-

The framing is made from 2 in × 1 in timber, screwed together, and covered in ½ in, chipboard or ply 6-12 mm thick, depending on the overall size of the baseboard.

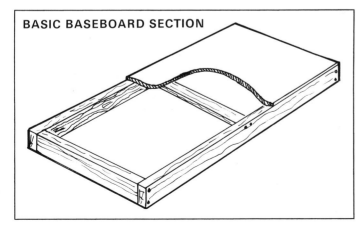

BASIC BASEBOARD SECTION

Layouts are best built up from a number of baseboards bolted together. This shows a few simple arrangements using standardised sections.

USING THE MODULES

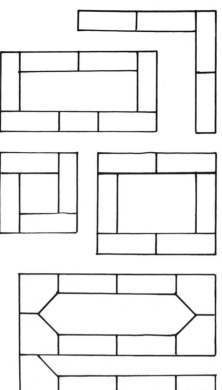

Simple baseboard framing from 2 in × 1 in timber, held together with coach bolts.

vealed that the simple framed baseboard, with plain butt joints, has an inherent weakness, for as anyone with any knowledge of design will appreciate, the whole strength of these joints is dependent on the holding powers of the screw plus the adhesion of the glue, if the sections are in fact so joined.

In theory, halved joints are better, providing you can make them accurately, which in practice either means you are an expert carpenter to begin with, or have invested in a Jointmaster or similar device.

A rather simpler answer is to reinforce the corners, either with small internal angle brackets—these are quite inexpensive, particularly if you can track down a store that sells them loose rather than in bubble packs—or, even easier, by the use of ply or hardboard gusset plates.

A word now about the top surfaces. Although, for some applications the softer wallboards may be used, experience shows that they can sag alarmingly. Therefore modern thought turns towards either 12 mm chipboard or ply.

Both materials appear to give good results, a great deal depends on one's individual preference and, let's be open about this, the ready availability of suitable supplies. There is the point that

whereas in chipboard, 12mm is the thinnest material available, 6mm ply, given a reasonable amount of bracing, is quite adequate for our purpose, indeed, for small, light systems, particularly intricate multi-level models, 4mm ply with adequate bracing is fine in expert hands.

Careful woodworkers may use halved joints, as shown, to increase strength. A good, inexpensive way of strengthening a corner is a ply gusset.

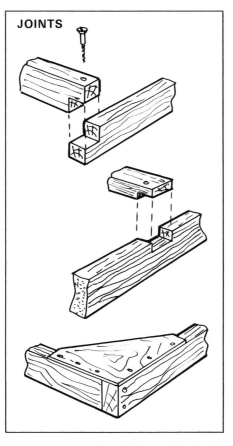

JOINTS

Ply is slightly the more noisy of the two, but much depends on the form of construction.

OPEN TOP

The traditional solid top baseboard is an excellent scheme in station areas, where most of the surface is covered by track at one level, but in open country, open top construction is to be preferred. Here the track is carried on a narrow strip of board, supported at fairly close intervals—around 9in to 12in intervals—by cross bracing. This cross bracing need not be the standard 2in×1in timber, 1in×$\frac{3}{4}$in will often suffice.

With open top construction it is easy to arrange for sections of the terrain to be below rail level, with considerable increase in realism. It frequently helps in such cases to lower the level of the framing, relative to the station areas. Dropping the framework by one inch gives greater freedom, but even more dramatic effects are achieved when the section is lowered a foot or more, creating a valley which demands a viaduct.

PLY FRAMES

There is only one reason for using 2in× 1in timber, it is relatively cheap, easy to obtain and does not carry a severe weight penalty. It is, however, too weak to allow for much more than a 4ft span, for this a deeper section is needed. In point of fact, the strength of a frame member depends far more on its depth than its thickness.

In this hobby, as in most others,

More cross bearings are needed to support the narrower sub-base. They can be notched to clear a low road or a river.

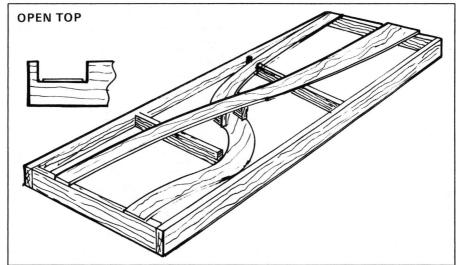

OPEN TOP

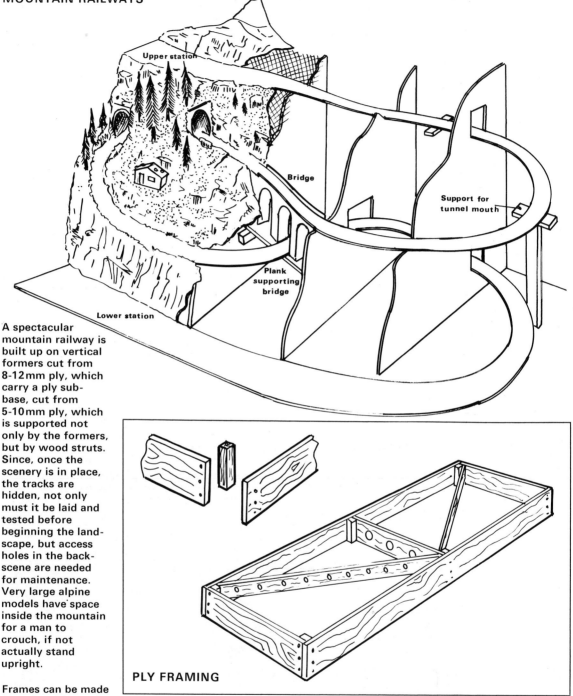

Upper station

Bridge

Support for tunnel mouth

Plank supporting bridge

Lower station

A spectacular mountain railway is built up on vertical formers cut from 8-12mm ply, which carry a ply sub-base, cut from 5-10mm ply, which is supported not only by the formers, but by wood struts. Since, once the scenery is in place, the tracks are hidden, not only must it be laid and tested before beginning the land-scape, but access holes in the back-scene are needed for maintenance. Very large alpine models have space inside the mountain for a man to crouch, if not actually stand upright.

Frames can be made from 8 or 12mm ply. A simple structure, with diagonal bracing is shown. Note the lightening holes in the bracing and the stiffening blocks at the joints.

PLY FRAMING

people come from all walks of life, and inevitably some are drawn from the boatbuilding and aeronautical industries. Applying their expertise, they realised that common deal is a pretty awful material anyway, and that plywood is far superior. The one inherent snag, that ply-wood comes in large sheets disappeared as soon as accurate power cutting tools became readily available, it is quite a simple matter to rip a sheet of ply into 3 in or 4 in deep frame members.

Furthermore, on a fully landscaped open top baseboard, the cross bracing can take the form of ply profiles. This is a fairly advanced concept, since the landscape must be accurately pre-planned, but this can readily be done if, at the end of the preliminary paper and pencil stage, a small scale model to a scale of 12 : 1 or 10 : 1 is built from card, balsa strip and modelling clay to prove the design. The completed model can be used as a visual check during all stages of construction.

A ply frame is similar in concept, but in general, it is the practice to join the sec-

tions with fillets of wood, usually around 1 in square. Furthermore, it is almost essential during construction to make good use of various clamps, in particular the very useful corner clamp. Since in this fairly advanced design, one knows that things are going to stay put, the use of a modern resin woodworking adhesive is recommended.

The important point about such a frame is that its strength to weight ratio is high. This can be still further improved by the addition of lightening holes.

Of these the most obvious occur in the cross members. It is perfectly practicable to remove most of the centre without in any way impairing the strength of the cross member. At the same time large holes, anything from 1 in to 2 in in diameter can be drilled in the side members. This, whilst of little importance in a permanent site, can be of prime consideration on a portable model. These lightening holes are practicable since,

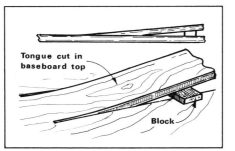

GRADIENTS
The accompanying photograph shows how gradients are built up, using a ply sub-base and graduated supports. It is vital to arrange a smooth start. One method is shown above, a tongue is cut in the baseboard surface, and then wedged up. Alternatively, begin the gradient with a long tapered wedge. A rise of 1 in in 30 in length is, for most purposes, the steepest climb that can be tolerated. The diagrams tend to exaggerate the slope for reasons of clarity.

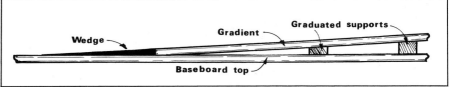

Where a baseboard is carried across a gangway a lifting flap is provided. The hinges must be mounted above rail level.

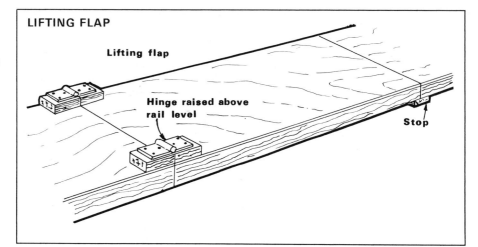

LIFTING FLAP

Lifting flap

Hinge raised above rail level

Stop

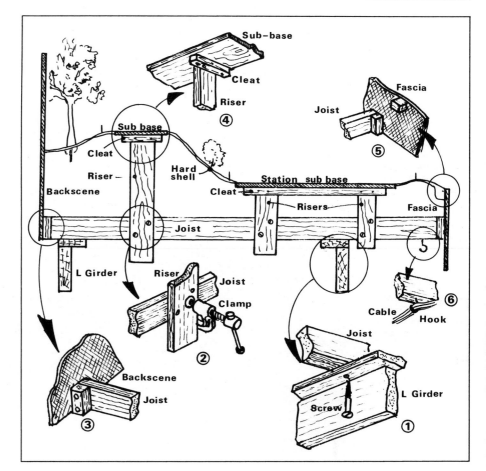

Sub-base

Cleat

Riser

④

Fascia

Joist

⑤

Sub base

Cleat

Riser —

Backscene

Hard shell

Cleat —

Station sub base

Risers

Fascia

Joist

L Girder

Riser

Joist

Clamp

⑤

Cable

Hook

⑥

Backscene

Joist

Joist

③

Screw

L Girder

①

②

L GIRDER DETAILS

1 The L girder is made from two lengths of wood glued and pinned. Joists are screwed from underneath.
2 Risers are held temporarily with a clamp to get gradients correct before screwing to the joist.
3 Backscene and fascia screwed to small cleats.
4 Top of rise, showing cleat.
5 Small wood blocks on fascia provide anchorage for plaster shell.
6 Cable runs are supported by hooks in joists.

when one regards the side member as a girder, the main function of the middle 2 in of a 3 in deep frame is to hold the stress bearing edges the requisite distance apart. The holes in the cross members provide clearance for wiring and possible mechanical point and signal control systems, whilst the holes in the side members, as well as allowing control wires to come out the side also provide useful, secure handholds. Light diagonal cross bracing can be added if desired to strengthen the structure.

LIFTING FLAPS

Such a structure has considerable appeal in certain applications, notably the lifting flap across the doorway or passageways of a permanent layout. The principle of the lifting flap is fairly obvious, anyone who has spent much time in the bar of a pub will have seen it in action. This is worth some study since it is obvious, in a pub, that anything placed on the bar flap has to be moved to permit access.

However, this immediately brings to mind Barnes Wallis' brilliantly simple geodetic construction. It is doubtful if there is any advantage in applying this system with its full rigour since it implies the use of a small number of precision-made structural members. The possibility of

L girder in use on a small layout. Note how the risers lift the track base and the road (to the rear). The fascia board indicates the proposed ground profile.

arranging cross members to form a triangulated frame, which is, as everyone must be aware, resistant to twist, is a high one and, with modern power woodworking machinery, does not really present overmany problems to the reasonably capable amateur and can help produce greater strength.

Oddly enough, some designers persist in placing sidings on lifting flaps. This is one area of a layout that can only carry running lines, though pointwork is not ruled out.

The important thing to bear in mind is the need to elevate the hinges above the top level of the track, or to use a special pattern offset pivot hinge of the type used in certain kitchen cabinet applications.

However, in mentioning lifting flaps we have got ahead of the important business of supporting our baseboard framing. Before we explore this, or the equally vital systems of framework joints, there is one novel system of baseboard construction we have to mention, and the question of sub bases must be explored.

L GIRDER

For a large, scenic layout, permanently housed in its own site, the American system of L girder construction is to be preferred. In essence, the conventional framework is deleted, two long frame members run the whole length and are supported on just four legs.

The frames are inverted L section. To these, joists are secured, normally, but not invariably, at right angles to the L girders. From the joists, risers go up to support the trackbeds which are secured by cleats. The diagram should make this clear.

Since all the framing is screwed together, and furthermore in true L girder practice, all screws are inserted from beneath and are thus fully accessible, modifications are simple. It is no longer the case that a cross member directly under the proposed position of a turntable well is a disaster, for all one does is move the offending member.

The American design calls for 3 in × 1 in main timber with 2 in × 1 in top. In the USA, lumber is cheap. In Europe, wood may grow in trees, but it doesn't grow *on* them. 3 in × $\frac{3}{4}$ in is ample, with a 1$\frac{1}{2}$ in × 6 mm ply top, which is nailed and glued to the vertical. There is no reason why the vertical should not be made from ply, or, for that matter, have a fish-belly section,

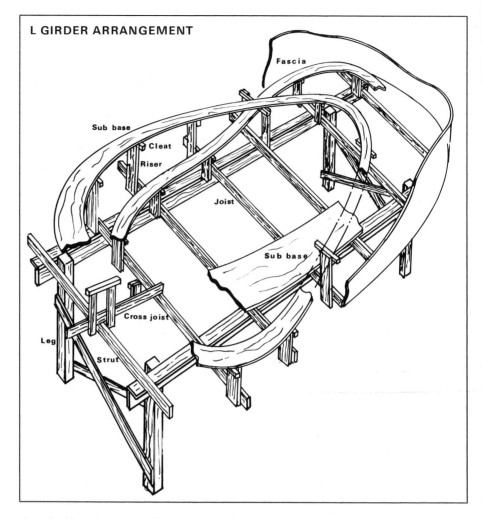

L GIRDER ARRANGEMENT

Fascia

Sub base

Cleat

Riser

Joist

Sub base

Cross joist

Leg

Strut

though this only matters if you can make good use of the offcut. On a normal permanent layout, the weight is not of primary importance.

The joists are secured from underneath. Legs can be kept to the absolute minimum. Furthermore, L girder principles are suitable for a Dexion or Handy-Angle baseboard frame.

It is worth mentioning that L girder construction can be carried out with timber of varying sections.

SUSPENDED AND HINGED BASEBOARDS

Weight could have some bearing, if the intention was to construct a layout which was suspended on pulleys from the ceiling. This particular approach is, in my opinion, only practicable in one situation, that of a garage with a fairly high roof. Few houses have sufficient headroom to

allow for a layout suspended in this fashion, but, even more to the point, it is not a good idea to have a large suspended weight over an area in which people foregather. The Sword of Damocles has nothing on this, that would just get one man, a suspended layout in a dining room could put the entire dinner party in hospital.

One scheme often canvassed is for a hinged baseboard against the wall. This is really only applicable to outright beginners, it is sound enough for youngsters, but it has, in an exaggerated form, the inherent snag of the bar flap—before you can lift it, everything has to come off. Furthermore, there is a very definite width limit.

Providing access can be arranged, the floor suitably strengthened and ventilation ensured, the loft is a good place for a permanent layout. In such a site, a novel form of construction is feasible, providing

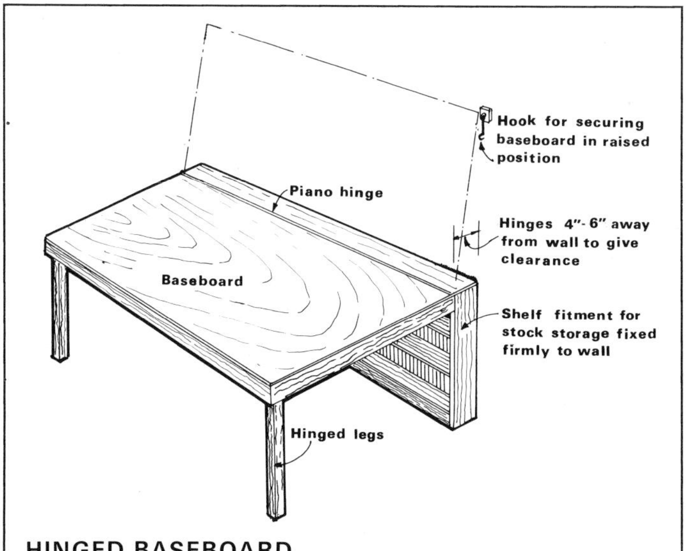

Hook for securing baseboard in raised position
Piano hinge
Hinges 4"-6" away from wall to give clearance
Baseboard
Shelf fitment for stock storage fixed firmly to wall
Hinged legs

HINGED BASEBOARD

Small layouts can be hinged against a wall. It is vital to provide firm fixing in the upright position.

careful pre-planning is the rule. Ply profiles, secured by screws to the rafters, can be cut. In order to level them, the front edge must carry a datum notch which is aligned to a taut cord which is trued with a spirit level. There is then only need for a profile board to link the front edges.

SUB BASES

Now this does pose one problem, laying track *in situ*. This brings us to the question of sub-bases.

The open top system of construction not only does away with the need to have solid timber across all the framing, it does away with the need to assemble the track and pointwork in position on the layout. As was pointed out earlier, while it is fairly easy to turn a baseboard section about on a workbench, it is even easier to turn a relatively small area of sub-base

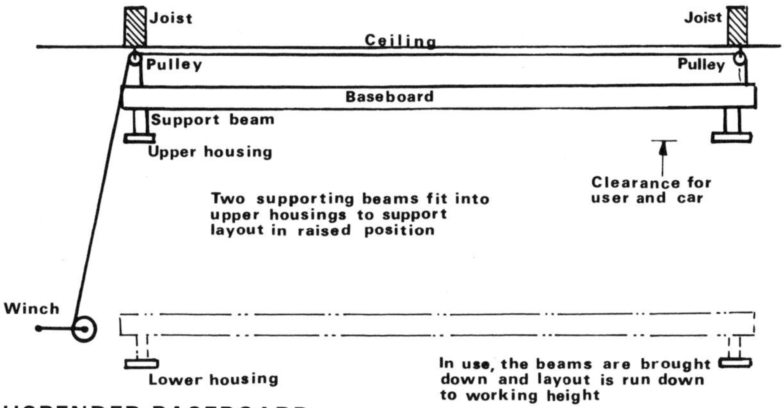

Joist
Joist
Ceiling
Pulley
Pulley
Baseboard
Support beam
Upper housing
Clearance for user and car
Two supporting beams fit into upper housings to support layout in raised position
Winch
Lower housing
In use, the beams are brought down and layout is run down to working height

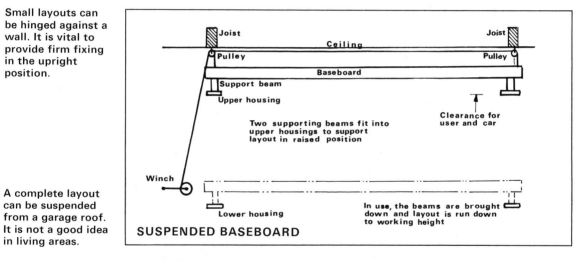

SUSPENDED BASEBOARD

A complete layout can be suspended from a garage roof. It is not a good idea in living areas.

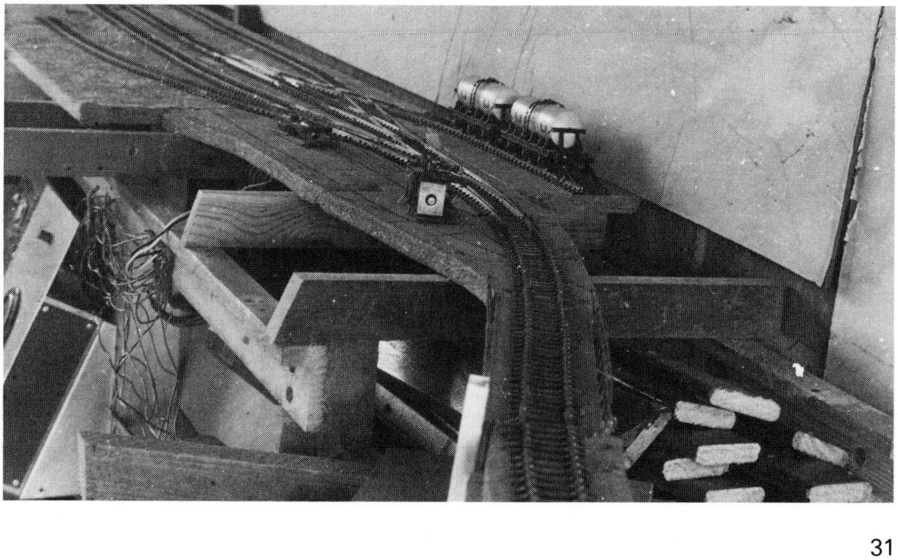

Even though this station is at one level, L girder construction has been adopted for its flexibility. The pointwork was installed on sub-bases.

end from end or upside down whilst you lay track in position.

It is, for absolute convenience, useful to have all sub-bases cut from material of the same thickness. This is by no means essential, since, with a little suitable packing, the thinner can be brought up to the same height as the thicker.

Although it might seem, at first glance, that the provision of pre-cut ply profiles would provide support for sub-bases, the provision of cleats permits not merely a fine adjustment in height, but allows the possibility of introducing cant on curved tracks. This only sounds complicated, in point of fact it is relatively simple, a matter of commonsense use of the quite considerable leeway implicit in any system of screwing two or more pieces of wood together.

JOINING BASEBOARDS

There are various methods available for joining baseboard sections together. Of late a great deal of play has been made of the virtues of precision alignment arranged by various proprietary fastenings. Yet, in practice, simple, inexpensive methods have given excellent service, providing they are used with a modicum of commonsense. Where baseboards remain erected for any length of time, the best, most reliable, and by far and away the easiest system of alignment is to hold the two sections together with a pair of coach bolts. This isn't absolutely precise, but on the odd occasion when there is serious misalignment—say as much as 1 mm—a sharp tap with the palm of the hand will ensure alignment.

If this sounds crude, it isn't. What many people fail to appreciate is that complication and sophistication are not necessarily elegance. The human eye, brain and hand, working together, give the greatest accuracy practicable within our parameters, because so long as we rely on timber, we accept dimensional instability.

However, coach bolts are slow acting and inconveniently located under the framing. For portable systems, two excellent jointing methods employ simple, inexpensive devices you can get in any DIY store.

One is an elementary dowelling system involving two screws. You start by drilling two holes in one end frame a close fit on a No. 8 woodscrew. If you like, you can determine precise centres for these screws relative to track centres, but in practice,

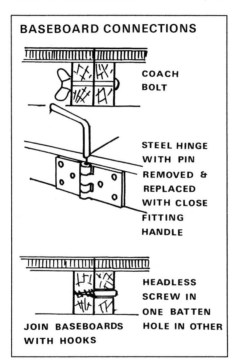

BASEBOARD CONNECTIONS

COACH BOLT

STEEL HINGE WITH PIN REMOVED & REPLACED WITH CLOSE FITTING HANDLE

HEADLESS SCREW IN ONE BATTEN HOLE IN OTHER

JOIN BASEBOARDS WITH HOOKS

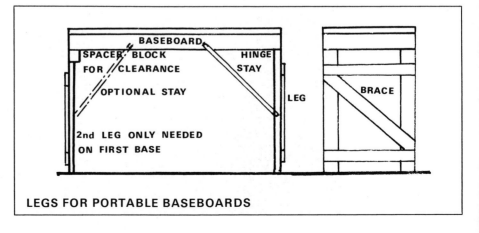

BASEBOARD

SPACER BLOCK FOR CLEARANCE

HINGE STAY

OPTIONAL STAY

LEG

BRACE

2nd LEG ONLY NEEDED ON FIRST BASE

LEGS FOR PORTABLE BASEBOARDS

More L girder construction at an early stage. The two joists running at an angle were to form part of a canal. The catch-as-catch-can methods of L girder construction are well brought out.

interchangeability is not of paramount importance, and the probability of making an error in measurement is high. Next clamp the sections together in alignment—take your time about this—then when you are satisfied all is correct, insert two No. 8 woodscrews long enough to go firmly into the second end member far enough to engage most, if not all of the threaded portion. If it is practicable, cut off the heads and separate the sections, if not, remove the screws, separate the sections, re-insert the screws carefully to preserve their alignment and then cut off the heads. Smooth the cut ends with a file and you have a pair of quite accurate dowels for a fraction of a penny. To hold these sections together, simple hooks and eyes can be used. A neat system employs a strip of metal and two round-head woodscrews. In theory this system can wear but it does not, in general, wear sufficiently to give any real trouble.

A very quick system of joining involves nothing more complex than a pair of flap back hinges. Remove the pins and replace with a close-fitting wire peg—a suitable

round nail is probably the best for this. Now screw firmly across the joint on each side. In use, remove the peg to dismantle, re-insert when you want to join. Originally, cast brass hinges were used, but as their price escalated it was discovered that the much cheaper bent steel pattern were quite accurate enough for our purpose. Actually, any hinge can do the job, but the flap back pattern gives a wider area for the fixing and seems more able to take the strain.

Another jointing device which is worth considering is the plastic screw-together fitting sold for the assembly of chipboard furniture. These have a pair of dowels and a metal screw fixing. In practice, for most applications, they are less convenient than a coach bolt and wing nut.

Legs are an important consideration. Some people talk of trestles, if you want to waste timber and add to your problems of level, they're sound enough, but adequate support is provided with a much simpler arrangement. For most conditions, a cross braced framework with 2×2 legs and $1\frac{1}{2}$in $\times \frac{1}{2}$in cross battens, accurately aligned and screwed firmly together is ample. It is vital to provide a number of struts, though on a permanent layout a common shelf bracket is much neater and rather stronger. On portable layouts, the usual practice is to hinge the legs to the framing. Only on the initial section to be erected is it necessary to have a pair of legs, subsequent baseboards only need one pair at the far end, support at the other being achieved by the adjacent baseboard.

BACKSCENES AND FASCIAS

Whilst not strictly part of the baseboard, backscenes and fascias need consideration. For these, hardboard is the preferred material; in the case of backscenes, it should be pinned to a light timber frame— 1 in × $\frac{3}{4}$ in is about right. It can be fixed to the framing, or made demountable, to taste. It is not a good idea to paint back-scenes on walls, even in a permanent lay-out room. Not only will you lose every-thing in the event of a move, but before you can sell the house you have to re-decorate the room!

The front fascia board isn't absolutely essential, but it neatens the edge. Further-more, on fully landscaped sections, the front edge will follow the profile of the countryside, whilst, in station areas, it often helps to raise the fascia slightly, partly to suggest a wall, partly to provide a means of catching derailed stock before it hits the floor.

Although hardboard is adequate, it really needs painting. A slightly more elegant solution is to cut the fascia from woodgrain effect plastic faced plywood, which is quite cheap, looks very good, even under close scrutiny, and, most im-portant of all, has a near permanent, smooth finish that can be kept clean with a wipe from a damp cloth.

Lighting

LAYOUT LIGHTING

It always helps to see what you are doing. More than that, if you want to get the colours on the layout to appear correct at all times, it is a good idea to begin by establishing a standard colour temperature for the model illumination.

At all events, the days when it was enough to rely on one single 100 watt lamp, without shade, suspended from a grimy length of twisted flex in the middle of the room are past. Whether the model is permanent or portable, good lighting is essential.

There are two favoured methods. The most elaborate, which is only suited for layouts that are likely to remain in position for a fair length of time, is to arrange a light framing above the model which incorporates a row of striplights. These can be fluorescent, tungsten, or a combination of both. The latter arrangement has the virtue that whereas fluorescent tubes are towards the cool, or blue end of the spectrum, tungsten are warm reddish yellow lights. Used together they come closer to true daylight. It should also be borne in mind that fluorescent lights are strong in ultra-violet light, which tends to cause fading with certain inks and water based paints. There is also the point that some people find fluorescent lights oppressive.

You should aim to flood enough light onto the baseboard to give enough light to permit hand-held photography. If you have access to an exposure meter, the ideal level is that of a light overcast day in early spring or late autumn, or around 1/60th second exposure at f8 with 64 ASA film if you want to be technical. For this you will need roughly 10 watts illumination per foot run of baseboard, depending on the efficiency of the light source and the distance from the layout. With strip lighting, shadowless illumination is more or less automatic.

For portable layouts, something simpler is required. Here the silvered spotlight comes into its own. A vertical batten fixed to the baseboard at any convenient position can carry up to four spotlights, which can be trained on strategic parts of the model. One of the paradoxes of our hobby is that we use far more electricity to see the trains move than we use to move them.

MODEL LIGHTING

The other aspect of light is the provision of illumination on the models. A good range of light fittings are now available,

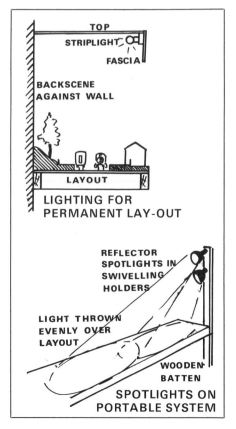

LIGHTING FOR PERMANENT LAY-OUT

SPOTLIGHTS ON PORTABLE SYSTEM

many of Continental origin. Prices tend to appear rather high, but if you try to model a lamp post, you will find out why. There are also plenty of miniature lamps available for building into your own models. One source, often neglected, is the cheap Christmas tree lighting set. There are, every year in the autumn, an array of such sets to be found in markets and cut price shops, of dubious origin and dubious safety. The lamps operate on around 12–16 V, and in cheap sets, the colour isn't very reliable either. Split up, these lamps work well on low voltage circuits.

However, before we go any further let's consider how lighting should be used. It is for primarily a night effect, it allows you to dim, or extinguish the main lights and turn on a mass of small lamps on the model. Unless yours is primarily an urban scene, then this is not for you, since where the model runs through open country away from built up areas, there would only be light from the occasional cottage.

It is a fact that most model lighting is far too bright. Artificial light cannot be seen in daylight at any distance. The normal miniature lamp, on 12–16 V supply, is more akin to the sort of lighting used for photography, it burns, moreover, at the blue end of the spectrum. Run the same lamp on between 6 and 8 V and it has a lovely golden glow. It also has a much longer life, it is reckoned that a 10 per cent drop in operating voltage doubles the life of a filament lamp, there is no effective data on the result of a 50 per cent drop, but inspired guesses put the life into years instead of hours. Since many lamps, once installed in a model building, are virtually inaccessible, this, is an important consideration. Unfortunately the best source of extreme low voltage at reasonable amperage, the heater transformers for mains operated thermionic valve radios and the like, is no longer so easily obtainable, but on the other hand, it is extremely rare for the transformer to be unserviceable on a scrap mains valve radio.

When we speak of small lamps, we have to realise that most of them are still very large. Oddly enough, the round torch bulb is the right shape and almost the right size to represent the old fashioned arc light, so for period models, this is a cheap and straightforward source of illumination. Many small lamps can be persuaded to look like the glass surround of a major light fitting but, without exception, they are all too big for a scale model gas lamp in 4 mm scale or smaller.

FIBRE OPTICS

This is where modern technology, in the shape of fibre optics, comes into the picture. Fibre optics can be seen in action in those kitsch light sprays. The same filaments, or similar ones of larger diameters, can conduct light from a single lamp under the scene to point light

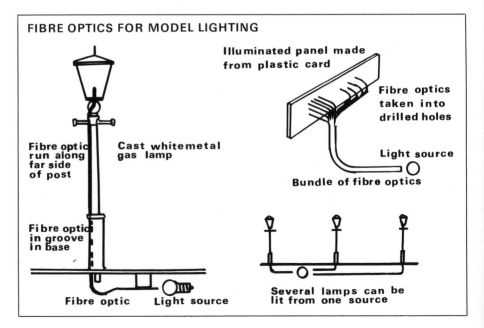

FIBRE OPTICS FOR MODEL LIGHTING

Illuminated panel made from plastic card

Fibre optics taken into drilled holes

Fibre optic run along far side of post

Cast whitemetal gas lamp

Light source

Bundle of fibre optics

Fibre optic in groove in base

Fibre optic   Light source

Several lamps can be lit from one source

sources. The business end can be lightly melted with the hot end of a soldering iron to form a small lens of sorts and produce a larger blob of light. Indeed, the possibilities with small lights and fibre optics are limited only by one's ingenuity and determination.

LED's

The latest form of illumination is the light emitting diode. At present it only comes in red, an odd green and a muddy amber, but it can be obtained in very small sizes. It operates on 3V DC, and accordingly is normally worked from 12V DC through a small dropping resistor, which is generally supplied with the LED. LED's are ideally suited for colour light manufacture, providing the operating voltage is not exceeded they have an indefinite life, they can be obtained in very small sizes.

A few German concerns, notably Busch, have developed LED lighting, and solid state technology to produce not merely festoons of lights for Christmas trees or garden barbecues (depending on the model season), but in a variety of situations where flashing lights are needed. The costs are high, particularly when complex solid state timing circuits are involved, but they are great fun and well worth considering as part of an eye-catching scene.

Tracklaying

A small OO gauge terminus throat laid with Peco Streamline, fixed direct to the ply baseboard top. Many hours work went into getting perfect alignment.

There is one simple, straightforward, economical answer to the whole business of tracklaying. It can be expressed in one word, Peco.

This British firm not only produces a complete range of flexible track for O, OO and N gauge, it exports this world wide where it is frequently preferred to the local product. Since it is also reasonably priced, for once in a while one can buy British in the quiet confidence that one cannot honestly do better.

The following method of tracklaying differs slightly from the manufacturer's instructions but has been tested in practice and is offered as an alternative.

The essence of the scheme lies in one simple fact, pointwork, using ready-made turnouts, is fixed in size and cannot be fiddled in any way without ensuring poor performance. It is the writer's considered opinion that every case of poor performance alleged with this track system arises because the user has either failed to grasp this, or has decided he knows better than the manufacturer, who stresses the importance of accurate alignment in the detailed instruction, sheet enclosed with every Peco point. So it is essential to pre-plan to full size, exercising full care.

PRE PLANNING

Preliminary planning can be carried out using the Peco point plans. These are full-size representations of the various turnouts, sold in a large sheet plan, which can be cut up and placed in position on the baseboard. Then, once the correct selection of turnouts have been determined and acquired, the next step is to start all over again.

Yes, start again. Unfortunately, although the point plans provide an accurate representation of the size, they do not necessarily line up automatically, and one can get them a few degrees out of alignment. This is asking for trouble on the actual pointwork.

So, take the points and the necessary joiners and put them together on a flat, level surface, then check the alignment by squinting along at rail level.

There is no better way of discovering infinitesimal kinks; it is, moreover, the favoured final check of the prototype ganger, even with today's sophisticated test equipment on full size railways.

INSTALLATION AND TESTING

Once you have aligned the pointwork *in situ*, either on the baseboard, or better still, the sub-base, mark the location of the tiebars, remove the pointwork and make provision for the point operating mechanisms of your choice. Now replace the pointwork and fix in place. Initially, only use a few fine trackpins and do not drive fully home, connect some lengths of track at each end and test.

Ideally, this is done by hooking the power supplies to the rails and running a locomotive over the points. However, most people are happy to run a wagon or a coach through. If this is done by gently tilting the base and allowing it to run through by gravity, all is well, pushing with the forefinger will not detect many forms of misalignment.

A sweeping approach to a station in N gauge, showing the value of large curved points.

Few point formations are made up wholly of turnouts and crossings, so small lengths of flexible track must be accurately cut to fit. It is absolutely essential that the fit must be precise to within $\frac{1}{2}$mm at the worst, it is well worthwhile backtracking and remaking an offending piece.

It will be found essential to cut away the ends of sleepers adjacent to the ends of turnouts, use a sharp craft knife. Use the same craft knife to cut away the fastening on the end sleeper to make room for the rail joiners, metal or insulated.

It cannot be over-emphasised that the turnouts and crossings must not be strained, and must be accurately aligned one with another. Unless this is done with scrupulous care, you will not get good running. Furthermore, it is essential that points lie flat on the baseboard or sub-base; in particular the point crossing or frog must be level with the adjacent rails.

Until you are satisfied that the points are perfectly aligned, do not drive the fixing pins home. If need be remove the pins and use another hole in the turnout for the fresh pin; this is one reason why we advised against fixing in every hole, because if a pin has gone in slightly skew, it will go on going in skew. Indeed, if there are enough plain track fillers in the formation, fix through these and leave the points held in place by the tracks alongside. If the worst comes to the worst, a few feet of track can be replaced at minimum cost and bother.

PLAIN TRACK

Laying plain track is simpler than pointwork, since it is possible to flex it to any reasonable curve.

There are two methods of establishing a true curve. One is a radial trammel, a system that is recommended in many textbooks. It certainly looks attractive, but frankly we have never seen it in successful operation since the trammel is, almost invariably, located in the middle of nowhere and, furthermore, the whole contraption gets in the way. In certain situations on a permanent layout one will find the centre of the curve located outside the walls!

A much better system is the provision of a series of curve templates which can be cut from hardboard, ply, card or plastic card. Commercial templates, sold under the name Tracksettas are also available in

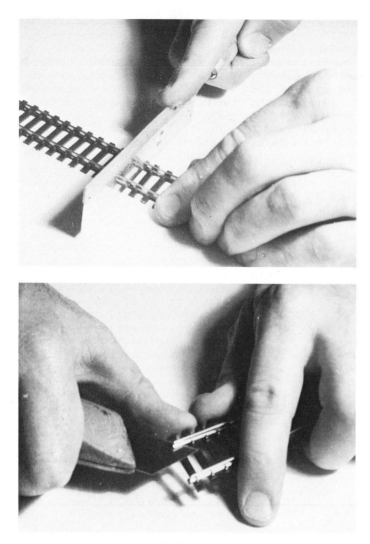

varying radii. In use the curved track is flexed against the template and pinned down methodically. Straight track may be laid against a template.

Cutting flexible track to length is not as difficult as it might seem. A simple cutting tool can be made from a piece of hardwood which has two grooves in the face to take the rails. It is held over the track in the left hand whilst the rails are cut through with a 6 in pin ended miniature hacksaw held in the right. Alternatively one may use a razor saw, but this tends to twist on the way through the rail and in any case is much slower and more expensive.

An alternative method of cutting rail is to use a small thin abrasive disc held in a low voltage drill. This is remarkably rapid and effective, but safety glasses should be worn to protect the eyes in the event of any chips or even bits of wheel flying in the face. While the risk is minimal, one's eyesight is too precious to leave to chance.

These miniature drills are very useful in tracklaying for not only will they gap rails, but they are the ideal instrument for drilling sleepers.

JOINING TRACKS

Tracks are secured together with rail joiners. These are rather longer than the usual fishplates and accordingly provide somewhat better electrical connection.

It is vital, therefore, to remove the rail fixings from the end sleeper before inserting the joiner so that the sleeper spacing may be maintained. Incorrect spacing can, of course, be rectified by inserting a loose sleeper under the joint, the trouble is that this is one of those jobs that somehow never gets done. Moreover, there is the snag that the loose sleeper lacks stability and needs a lot of

(Top) Cutting flexible track with a razor saw.

(Above) Cutting away rail fixing at at ends of the track section.

Joining tracks. The top way is wrong, with an unsightly sleeper gap. The lower picture shows how it should be done.

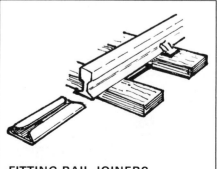

FITTING RAIL JOINERS

Pointwork mounted on a ½ in chipboard sub-base. This unit was built wired and tested on the workbench before installation on the layout. This ensured that it was in good order from the start: it stayed that way. The start of a rising grade for a branch can be seen behind.

fixing if it is not to move out of place. It is much simpler to remove the rail fixings.

SUB ASSEMBLIES

In most layouts you will find that 80 per cent of all pointwork occurs in a few complexes, usually at each end of the station. One great virtue of the open top and L girder systems is that these complexes can be mounted permanently on a small sub-assembly measuring no more than 2 ft × 1 ft on average. These assemblies carry 80 per cent of turnouts and point motors, they also have around 90 per cent of the electrical connections.

By doing all this work on a sub assembly it becomes a perfect bench job. The sub assembly can readily be turned end for end, even inverted to work on the point motors, all the wiring can be installed and checked under optimum conditions, in comfort. Not only is it easy to assemble, it is easy to dismantle this vital part of the layout and re-use it on another site.

For convenience, all wiring should be connected to a tag strip by about two to three feet of multi-core cable, either bought as a cable or made up from a number of strands of wire. The details of wiring must be entered into your wiring book and kept on hand.

A layout built in this fashion is in practice a very large sectional train set. It is also worth pointing out that this arrangement is particularly suited to layout construction in such awkward places as a loft, where it is extremely difficult to fit lay track accurately in the restricted headroom.

INSULATED JOINERS

It is necessary to have insulating joints in the rails for electric isolation. Plastic rail joiners, provided with a small central lug to prevent the rails accidentally touching, can be used, so it is advisable to plan the circuits before tracklaying begins. They are used in place of the normal metal joiners.

It is difficult to cut fresh isolating gaps with a saw after the tracks are laid, but if one has a mini-drill with abrasive disc, gapping is quite simple. With tracks on sub bases it is just possible to gap a rail by drilling a hole beside the rail and cutting through the rail with a piercing saw blade held in a fretsaw frame.

To prevent accidental contact between gapped rails fill the joint with an epoxy resin, such as Araldite. This not only acts as an efficient insulator, it will additionally assist fixing the ends of rails.

FIXING

We have, throughout, spoken lightly of fixing the track to the base. Now is the time to consider this in more detail.

The fine pin recommended by Peco is only suitable for use with a pulpboard or insulation board base. The inexplicable insistence on this somewhat weak and unreliable baseboard surface, which requires considerable bracing beneath to prevent it warping (in practice closer than the 12 in advised) is one side reason why some people have trouble with this excellent trackage system.

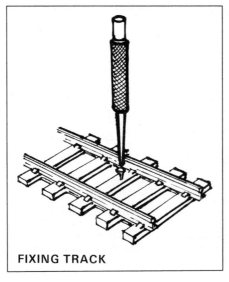

FIXING TRACK

To fix the track to chipboard or ply, fine veneer pins are needed. They fit neatly into the holes in the turnouts, and whilst they can be driven through the soft flexible plastic of the track sleeper base, it doesn't hurt to drill a small hole beforehand. Here the mini-drill will prove invaluable.

Initially, the pins should be driven down to about 1 mm above the sleepers, slightly below rail level. They should not be driven home until you are satisfied the track is properly aligned and correctly levelled, for once flush with the sleeper tops it becomes much more difficult to extract them. For this latter purpose a small pair of side nippers will act as miniature pincers.

Whilst the pins can be partially driven in with a light hammer, they must be driven home with a small flat faced pin punch. Do not hammer hard, a few light taps will suffice.

BASEBOARD JOINTS

It is vital that tracks should be aligned accurately across baseboard joints. Of all the ways of achieving this, nothing quite equals the utter simplicity of laying track straight across the gap and subsequently cutting the break with a saw.

To preserve alignment it is, in many cases, sufficient to pin the end sleeper down firmly. For added security, solder the rail ends to small woodscrews driven into the top surface, or replace the end sleepers with gapped PCB sleepers pinned to the base and soldered to the rail.

Where the layout is more or less perma-

nently erected, further security can be obtained by fitting rail joiners across the joint. In this instance it is generally best to cut away two fixings on one side so the joiners can be slid back before dismantling.

Another dodge for semi-portable systems is to have short sections of track loosely fitted across baseboard joins. Here the use of slid back rail joiners is normally essential, but some enthusiasts employ snap fasteners sold for dressmaking to provide a firm connection. The main fault with this arrangement is the difficulty of effective ballasting. Much depends on the period during which the layout is erected, for it is possible to apply loose ballast and remove this when the layout is dismantled. It means extra work, however.

Needless to say, you cannot have points straddling a baseboard gap. Furthermore, attractive as this might seem, do not have electrical isolating gaps at baseboard joins. It is all too easy for the rails to touch and create a short circuit. It helps to slightly radius the inside of the rails at a baseboard joint.

ELECTRICAL CONNECTIONS

It is necessary to connect the electrical feeds to the track, not only for the main feeds, but for isolating sections as well. Since we are trying to build a realistic railway the wiring should be as near invisible as possible, and the plug-in connecting clips used in the elementary ready-to-run system are not satisfactory.

There is no difficulty in carrying the major part of all wiring beneath the baseboard, One very good method is to drill a hole about $\frac{1}{16}$ in dia alongside the rail at the point where the feed is to be made, then take a length of bare copper wire of about 22 SWG roughly

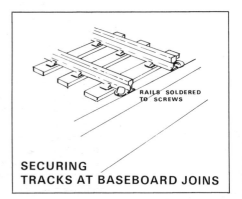

RAILS SOLDERED TO SCREWS

SECURING TRACKS AT BASEBOARD JOINS

This O gauge terminus has only just progressed beyond the plain track stage.

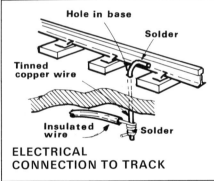

ELECTRICAL CONNECTION TO TRACK

1 in long. The last $\frac{1}{8}$ in is bent at right angles, then joggled as shown so that it lies snugly in the web of the rail. The rail must be clean at this point, a quick scrape with the end of a small screwdriver makes certain.

There is some slight difficulty persuading the wire to stay put, one method that does work well is to apply a small piece of paste flux, about the size of a lead shot, to the end of the wire, the stickiness of the flux keeps the wire in place.

The soldering iron must be hot, it should have a little solder on the tip and then be placed against the wire. The solder will then flow round the wire and into the web of the rail in a matter of seconds.

Don't leave the soldering iron lingering on the rail for long.

Do not solder feeds to points, if it is essential to take them to the toes of two points face to face, then solder to the rail joiner instead.

The main feed wires can be soldered to the bare ends of wire projecting below the baseboard. A quick twist of the wires will hold them in place while this is done.

Where it is undesirable to do this, push the feed wire up from underneath and solder this direct to the rail. This is rather important if the layout is permanently erected and the tracks are laid *in situ*. Soldering upward above one's face is not a very good idea at all.

THE FINAL JOINT

There used to be, in the USA, the business of the gold spike. This was driven in, with some ceremony when the last rails were joined and, presumably removed rather rapidly afterwards and sold as a souvenir. It was unlikely to have actually been gold, which is a lovely, but extremely ductile metal which would not take kindly to being hit with a sledgehammer!

While this has nothing to do with model railways directly, when tracklaying there are many situations where it is necessary to fix a length of track between

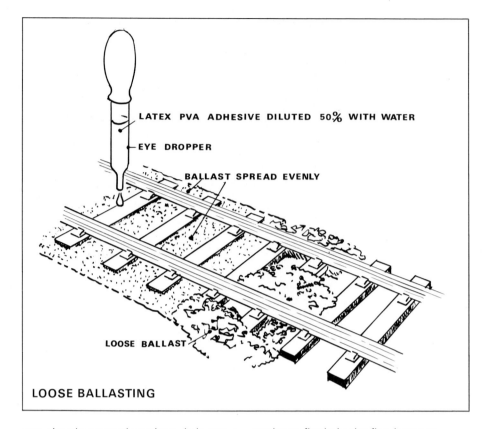

LATEX PVA ADHESIVE DILUTED 50% WITH WATER

EYE DROPPER

BALLAST SPREAD EVENLY

LOOSE BALLAST

LOOSE BALLASTING

two already secured sections. It is not a good idea to try to spring the rail joiners in place.

The correct method is to cut away *two* sets of rail fixings at the end of one track and to slide the rail joiners fully on the rail. Thus, they do not protrude beyond the end of rails and once the tracks are in place they can be slid in position.

LIFTING AND RELAYING TRACK

It is possible to lift flexible track and pointwork providing great care is exercised removing any pins from sleepers. However, with the best care in the world some damage may occur.

The commonest is undoubtedly the burring of sleepers where pins are extracted. It is possible to remove any badly damaged ones by cutting away the linking web beneath the rail and tearing out the damaged sleeper. The adjacent lengths of sleepering are then slid together. While a little rail will protrude, this small loss can be accepted.

A similar treatment is not possible with points, but here the more rigid sleeper base is less readily damaged. This is the reason we advised against fixing point-

work too firmly in the first instance.

Damaged rails are more difficult to deal with. A bad kink can only be removed by drastic surgery. In order words, cut the rails on either side of the kink.

RE-USING TRACK

Providing a length of track is in good order, it can be re-used on any section of the layout. However, it is not a good idea to use a lot of short sections on a running road, these can be reserved for siding use, or kept to employ as short fitting pieces between sections of pointwork.

This is more or less in accord with full size practice, but the reason is different, it is length and alignment rather than wear. Joins do make smooth alignment more difficult to achieve, and a smooth, evenly flowing running road is more readily achieved with sections of track over 18 in in length.

With odd lengths of track, some fall off in the running qualities may occur, and again, in sidings this is of less importance. On the prototype many sidings are in such bad condition that derailments are not so much an accident as a statistical certainty. Ours should improve upon this.

BALLASTING

Peco supply a foam plastic ballast underlay which is intended to give a cushioned ride—the floating track system in fact. For my part, I am not sold on this idea, though I admit many people prefer it. In my experience, it frequently produces some odd effects and certainly makes it virtually impossible to maintain accurate top—to use the correct railway term—on the tracks.

I advise loose ballast, either granulated cork or fine sieved rock. Coarse sand is a fair substitute, once painted. I do not advise mixing this with glue to form a paste. Applying ballast in this fashion is tedious and messy, it has given loose ballasting a bad name.

Apply the ballast dry, spread to the full depth of the sleepers and carefully tidy the edges to the correct width. When you are satisfied that this has been properly done, take a mixture of 50 per cent white PVA glue and 50 per cent tap water with one drop of washing up liquid added to make the solution flow more readily. Then, with an eye-dropper saturate the ballast with this adhesive. Leave overnight to dry.

The result is a hard, secure mass of ballast. It is possible to touch in after the main bulk is dry, for even with the utmost care, one usually discovers on final inspection a few places where the ballast hasn't gone where it should.

OTHER TRACKS

Although we have been speaking of Peco track, there are many other, less well known, less readily available forms of flexible track. Additionally, several ready-to-run manufacturers provide flexible track to fit in with their standard sectional tracks. These trackage systems are very good, their weakness, in general, is that their turnouts are too small a radius, and nothing like the superb Peco large radius turnouts is available.

However, because these, and the majority of modern sectional tracks for 16.5 and 9 mm gauges are made to uniform International standards, it is feasible to mix them on the one layout. Indeed, where the track radii required are pro-

Conrad sectional 16.5mm gauge track. Ready ballasted, with large radius curves available, and with small section rail, this is a quickly laid, high quality track.

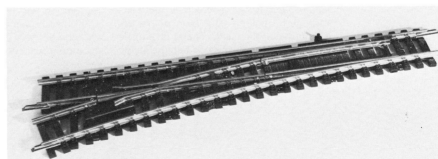

A Fleischmann 'high speed' turnout, giving a closed frog for smoother running.

Hand-made trackwork: a somewhat complex crossing.

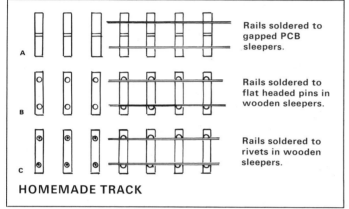

A	Rails soldered to gapped PCB sleepers.
B	Rails soldered to flat headed pins in wooden sleepers.
C	Rails soldered to rivets in wooden sleepers.

HOMEMADE TRACK

vided within a pre-formed sectional track system, it is a very good idea to use these rather than attempt to curve flexible track to very sharp curves.

You will also discover several tracks provided with smaller section rail; these have improved appearance, but there is the disadvantage that ready-assembled turnouts are not available, and thus one must use kits.

MAKING YOUR OWN

It is possible to construct your own track. The only snag is that the cost for plain track is little, if any different, generally any difference works to the advantage of ready-made track! There is a price advantage in making your own pointwork, if you have the skill. There is another advantage, the trackwork can be tailor-made for the situation and accordingly give far better results.

The favoured method today is to solder the rails to sleepers cut from printed circuit board (PCB), gapped down the centre for two rail insulation. Points are built on sleepers cut from long lengths of PCB, the gaps must be made by the builder.

It is not proposed to go into this system in any detail. Probably the best advice is to begin by purchasing a point kit, and learn from this. Although there is no doubt that the manufacture of plain track is much simpler, if you can't make the turnouts, as indicated, there is little point in making plain track. The work involved is considerable.

THE FINISHING TOUCHES

It is advisable to paint the sides of the rails. Although 'rail colour' can be bought, the actual colour varies from the blue-brown of newly laid track to a dirty, greasy off black on older sections of the line. This is a good way to use up old dirty paint!

Similarly, ballast is rarely the dark grey of granite. For a start, not all sections of British Railways use granite, a great deal of crushed limestone is employed. In earlier days, gravel, shingle and even ash was used. In steam depots, the top surface was usually ash.

Painting track with a brush is both time and brush consuming. The correct tool is an airbrush, here the simplest and cheapest model will suffice.

Platforms & People

The standard British railway station is provided with one, two, or in the case of a major station, several standard British raised platforms. Only, when you come to look at them, they aren't all that standard.

For a start, although all the textbooks tell you that they are 3 ft 0 in above rail level, this is in practice, the maximum height and, more often than not, stations fall short of the maximum by several inches. Whilst this is of little interest for most of us, there are two much lower levels in use, first for the London Transport tube lines, where the height is generally little more than a foot, and the so called 'compromise' height where tube and surface stock run on the same tracks, around 2 ft 3 in in practice. Then, older stations have a pleasing trick of being arranged at more than one level.

Then there are various methods of building the correct type, both on the prototype, and on the model. We will particularise.

TYPES

Modern platforms usually have cast concrete edging. The bit behind is filled with hardcore and then given a tarmac surface. There is a concrete slab edging. It is a very effective method, well suited to modern constructional techniques.

Before this, it was usual to construct a dwarf wall and top it with paving slabs. The top of the wall could be quite elaborate at times. Furthermore the platform surface might well be paving slabs, or even special large diagonal grooved bricks. On less important stations, and frequently, at the ends of the platforms, the surface would be gravel.

Another form of edging, very old, was plain brick with a brick top edging. Here

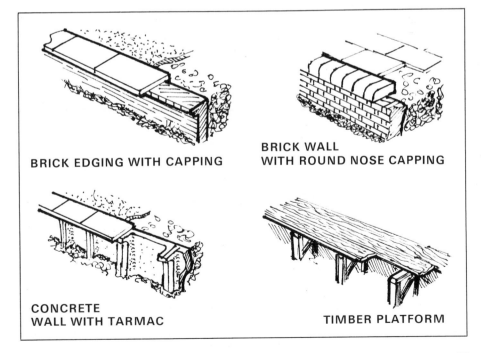

BRICK EDGING WITH CAPPING

BRICK WALL WITH ROUND NOSE CAPPING

CONCRETE WALL WITH TARMAC

TIMBER PLATFORM

Timber extension to stone platform on this OO layout.

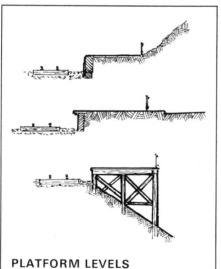

PLATFORM LEVELS

These sections show how prototype platforms relate to the lie of the ground.

there was no overlap, just a bullnosed brick course on edge.

Then there were timber platforms. These are gradually disappearing, partly because of the price of timber, partly because of the cost of erecting them. They were very popular around the turn of the century and were frequently used to extend earlier platforms.

It is by no means unusual to find a platform with two types of construction. In such cases the older pattern is always nearest the station buildings.

One important point to note, except where the railway runs along an embankment or brick arches, the platform is normally at ground level or even below, it is not, as on a toy train set, raised from the roadway. Exceptions can be found, but in most cases one either walks straight onto platforms from the approach road, or an extensive flight of steps is involved. Don't take our word for it, go and look at the full size railway.

CONSTRUCTION

Having said all that, the actual construction of a model platform is relatively easy! There are two basic methods, involving solid or frame construction.

Providing you can find a suitable piece of wood or man-made board of the right thickness, the solid system is simplest. There is a little work involved in shaping the board, that is all. Moreover, it is an excellent way of producing not only the platform, but also the station approach, complete with pavement and kerbstones.

The top surface can be a sheet of hardboard, smooth side up. It is not unduly difficult to carve the edge into coping stones. The longitudinal groove is easiest made with a carpenter's marking gauge, the joints between the stones cut with a craft knife, using an engineer's square to ensure that they are at right angles. Spacing can be set out with dividers. A little judicious fraying of the edges aids realism.

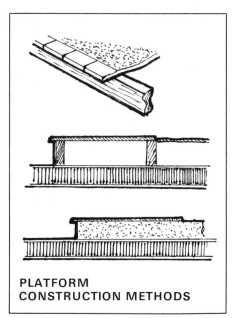

PLATFORM CONSTRUCTION METHODS

Alternatively, the paving stones can be made from plastic sheet. Slaters do two sizes of paving stone in large sheets. This can be cut as required, but for additional realism, the individual slabs may be readily broken along the grooves and then stuck back in position. Whilst this might seem very tedious, it creates the slightly irregular appearance of old paving, and will allow a high degree of individuality. Obviously, this sort of treatment is best suited to a small station, one would be very determined—and have a good deal of spare time to hand—to contemplate tackling a four platform station capable of handling eight coach trains in this manner.

It is also possible to construct the platform on a framework. This can be of card, wood or plastic card. Except on grounds of expense—for considerable quantities would be needed, plastic card is ideal, not only for its ease of working, but because one would make the top surface from the same material.

CURVED PLATFORMS

The only thing one has to watch about curved platforms is providing sufficient clearance for all stock. Marking out is surprisingly easy. Take a piece of thin card and cut to fit roughly along the ends of the sleepers. Now take your longest

A simple halt with post and rail fencing.

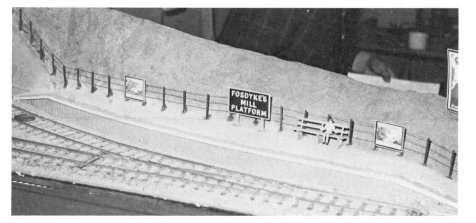

To mark out the correct curve for a platform, place a pencil against a coach side and run it along the track.

CURVED PLATFORMS

(Top) Station lamp and fencing provide the finishing touches on Richard Chown's Irish broad gauge layout in 7mm scale, Castle Rackrent.

(Above) A selection of figures by Merit.

White plastic letters on black plastic back, with white surround.

coach and place a slim pencil or a ballpoint refill vertically against the middle for interval curves and the end for external curves and run the vehicle back and forth, making a mark. Then check again, using an outside cylindered loco. Now cut out the card, mount on wood blocks and check for clearance at the platform height. Adjust as necessary then use this card to mark out your platform.

STATION NAME

TIMBER PLATFORMS

The modelling of timber platforms is a trifle time consuming, since one follows strict prototype practice. First the supports are cut from stripwood, generally balsa strip, as sold for model aircraft construction. Then, when these are up and have been suitably stained to resemble creosoted timber, planks cut from thin sheet wood—the veneers sold for marquetry are ideal—are fitted to the top one by one. Study of prototype photographs shows that whilst most timber platforms had the planking running parallel with the tracks, a few, particularly those with curves, were at right angles.

PLATFORM FURNITURE

A platform needs to be dressed up to look realistic. A lot depends on the period chosen, but some things remain un-

Cast platform slot machines.

FIGURES
A fine pin in one leg, fitting in a drilled hole on the platform, obviates the need for a 'slab base.

changed over best part of a century. Of these, the timber paling fence is the most prominent. Posters on boards are much easier now that several concerns—Tiny Signs are the largest—provide true scale replicas of authentic posters.

Seats, platform machines, trolleys and the like are manufactured and can be bought in any good model shop. There are a variety of miniature lamps on sale. The inexpensive plastic variety are nowhere near as realistic as the cast versions, which really do look like the old fashioned cast iron lamp post. Fibre optics can pro-

vide illumination.

Many stations has flowerbeds, indeed prizes were awarded to the best kept stations, and competition was stiff, not so much for the award, but because it was an excellent way of bringing oneself to the notice of superiors and getting selected for promotion to a more important station.

Last of all, passengers are needed. It is a good idea to remove any bases before cementing or pinning the figure in place. Unless you've run foul of the Mafia, you don't stand *in* a paving slab.

Wiring The Layout

WIRING TECHNIQUES

For most people wiring is a chore, to be got through as quickly and expeditiously as possible. Except on the simplest of systems, this is asking for trouble, since in the probable event of making a modification, the ease with which the wiring can be amended often determines how much change one can accommodate. A sound, consistent technique is to be advised. Above all, it is advisable to make some record of what you have done so that you can make alterations when needed. For most cases, a wiring book is the most straightforward answer. This is not a series of wiring diagrams, the nature of model railway wiring ensures that a wiring diagram consists of innumerable parallel lines and is difficult to read. The purpose of a wiring book is mainly to record the start and end of each piece of wire.

TAG STRIP

The key to successful layout wiring is the tag strip. There are various designs, all primarily intended for electronic use. All consist of a series of convenient solder tags on an insulating strip which provide a point where wires can be conveniently connected.

An alternative, somewhat more expensive, are the multiple screw connectors to be found in general stores, DIY shops and electrical suppliers. The latter are frequently able to sell them out of boxes at something approaching half the price of bubble packed equivalents in the chain stores. They are particularly suited for locations where one is likely to wish to make additional connections, or where for one reason or another, a soldering iron would be a nuisance.

In use tag strips are located at strategic places around the layout. The most obvious is the rear of the control panel. Here matched pairs of tag strips enable one to connect the panel to the layout with ease. Smaller tag strip assemblies are located at the principal wiring points around the system.

It is essential to number tag strips so that the function of each terminal can be recorded in the wiring book. Whilst it might seem advisable to number every one, in practice it is merely necessary to indicate which tag begins the numbering sequence. On very large arrays, clearly intermediate numbers are needed, and furthermore you must always number from left to right, or from top to bottom, these are the conventional arrangements

(Below) Tag strip at the end of a multi-core cable.

(Bottom) Tag strip for layout wiring. The wires have yet to be collected into a neat cable.

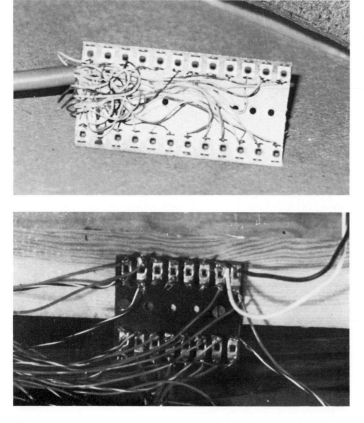

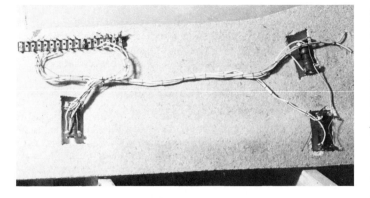

A tangle of wires is converted to this neatly cabled array in a few minutes.

and less easily forgotten. Needless to say, consistency is advisable, numbering in a random way creates extreme difficulties.

As an alternative, you can allocate each circuit a number, and then number each tag with its code. The system is used in industry, but depends for its success on a system of identifying each wire and is, in amateur use, rather more difficult to sustain.

COLOUR CODING

One of the more seductive ideas in wiring is to use different coloured wires for specific functions. Like all seductive ideas, it usually leads to heartache.

There are snags. The first is that there are, in general, more functions than simple colours, and while two-coloured wires are obtainable, they are not, except by stripping multi-core cables, that easily found.

Then quite a few model railway circuits have ambiguous functions, the more complex the control arrangements, the more likely a particular circuit can take its supply from at least three alternative supplies. So unless one utilises the same colour for three control circuits—which does rather diminish the function of colour coding—the only answer is to introduce a further colour. And another after that!

The final, and most telling argument against colour coding is its propensity for breakdown. The reason is simple, a model railway uses a good deal of wire. The logistics of supplying enough of every colour in use are formidable. It is a simple fact that one runs out of a specific colour when the suppliers are closed. This is not an application of Murphy's law, it is the simple consequence of the fact that most modelmaking is done outside shop hours, and although an exception is Saturday, the only individual who runs out of wire

on Saturday afternoon is one who forgot to check his stocks before beginning work. So, sooner or later, one finds oneself short of brown wire and with plenty of green, and faced with the alternative of waiting at least a day, or completing the wiring (which remember, is a chore to begin with) and getting the trains to run, which is the object of the exercise, the colour code goes by the board.

MULTIPLE CABLING

There is one area where colour coding does play its part. On any layout of size, there are cases where anything from six to sixty wires run together in a cable for some distance. If you can put in one wire at a time, all well and good; but when it is essential to link two tag strips over a yard apart, this can be timewasting, since one has to move from end to end, *carrying a hot soldering iron*. It is much more convenient to loop all the wires in at one end, then move to the other and connect up. In such a case, the use of a different colour for each wire ensures that you can sort the tangle out at the other end.

Even better, the use of a multi-core cable, which is naturally colour coded, makes this business even simpler. There are three types of multi-core cables. First is a flat, multi-coloured strip, which is economical. Next come the sheathed types, which generally cost a little more and can be obtained with a flexible core. Finally there are ex-GPO cables.

This last category needs special mention because if you happen to be in the right place at the right time it can be picked up for the asking—the right place being during extensive alterations to an office or works phone system. They have a couple of special features.

They use single core cable, and, because phone circuits use low currents, it is small in cross section. For this reason most users tend, except for relay circuits, to double up.

This is aided because, except for the basic four core wire used for a normal phone circuit, GPO cable is paired, that is to say each colour has an adjacent white lead, which, when you bare a couple of inches, will be seen to be wrapped round its colour. It is a good idea to check continuity at each end, just to be sure you've not crossed your whites. GPO engineers aren't prepared to proceed without checking, and they're fully trained.

MULTI- OR SINGLE-STRAND?

Wire comes in two varieties, single strand or multi-strand. The latter is essential for any situation where the wire must flex, i.e., for the connections between baseboards, or between control panels and the layout where the former are intended to be moved about.

Single core wire must always be regarded as fixed, too much flexing will lead to a fracture. However, since the majority of model connections are not subject to excessive movement, the single-core wire is generally more convenient.

Multi-core wire is very prone to fray at the ends when one is fitting it into tag strip, and almost impossible to prevent splaying out in an unsightly blob when used to connect to the track. This can be ameliorated by twisting the freshly stripped wire and soldering the wires together to form a solid mass stiff enough to stay put.

However, the prime consideration should be price and availability. It should be stressed that there is no such animal as 'layout wire'. What you require is low-voltage wire, which is used for a multitude of purposes. Generally speaking, 22 SWG single core, or something close to this, is needed. Very thin wire, in track and point motor circuits leads to excessive voltage drop and loss of power over anything but the shortest of distances.

STRIPPING WIRE

It is necessary to remove the plastic insulation from the wire. This is fairly obvious, but there are ways and ways. What you must not do is to cut the wire core. Even a small nick produces a weak point, and one common cause of trouble is a break at the extreme end of a wire. This is the more infuriating because such a break is rarely easy to spot.

You should always use proper wire strippers. We are nearly all supplied with a very effective pair, the notch between the two front upper teeth. However, this is very much an emergency arrangement, for the simple reason that it is often very awkward to get down to the wire.

Proprietary wire-strippers are sold. There is one type, which is found at the end of some screwdrivers which is designed to drag the insulation off. It doesn't work very well. The type which have an adjustable notch, which is set just to clear the wire core, are to be preferred. Of the lot, the most complex and costly, the special plier type, with a fine screw adjustment, seem in practice to be the most convenient, not only can you get the precise clearance you need, but because the stripping action is a straight pull, their use is more straightforward. This is very much the case when working in confined spaces.

CABLE RUNS

Insulated wire never has been exactly cheap, and since a model railway can soon use up several hundred yards, there is a natural impulse to take the wires straight from point to point by the most direct route. Except on the simplest of schemes, this is false economy, because it produces a complete cat's cradle which effectively prevents access to anything under the baseboard.

Good practice carries all wiring in cable runs. This usually means that most wires are at least 10 per cent longer than the direct route, but that they are neatly taken along a path where the possibility of their getting in the way is minimal. Furthermore, by providing a little slack, it is possible to reconnect the ends, either

(Below) Two patterns of wire strippers.

(Bottom) A selection of miniature switches for controls.

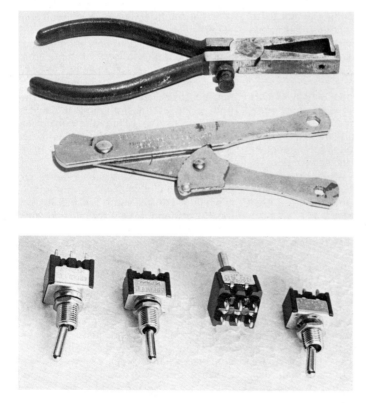

Cabled wiring to
point relays.

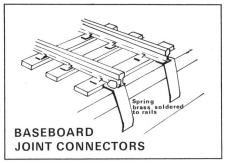

Spring
brass soldered
to rails

**BASEBOARD
JOINT CONNECTORS**

chases switches through regular suppliers, model shops and electronic component suppliers are the main sources, they also can be found in surplus stores. Whilst it is now a good decade since the vast outpourings from World War II surplus sales finally disappeared, and the dingy little Aladdin's caves of inexpensive components, and wonderful gadgets that turned out to be white elephants finally gave up the ghost, there are still a few concerns which have stocks of recently purchased equipment for sale at under half the price of new. However, in the surplus market, experience is essential if one is not to waste money.

BASEBOARD CONNECTIONS

One perennial problem is the connection between baseboard sections. There are two separate situations, the permanently erected layout which is liable to be dismantled on occasions, and the portable or semi portable system which is taken up and down at frequent intervals.

Where the layout is only intended to come down in emergencies, wiring is best carried across joins between pairs of tag strips. When a move is indicated, the short intervening wires are simply cut. However, if the move, whilst infrequent, is regular, it is better to use screw pattern connectors for it is slightly easier to reconnect.

Where disconnection is fairly common, multi-pin plugs and sockets are needed. Two patterns are popular, the Jones plug, which has fairly heavy flat pins, and the octal plug and socket, which had its origins in the obsolescent thermionic valve. Another type of plug and socket is the DIN pattern, mainly used for audio work. The main failing here is the relative paucity of circuits available.

There are large multi-pin connectors used in printed circuit technology. In general, unless you can find both plug and socket in a surplus store they tend to be expensive.

A very simple system which works well on true portable systems is made up from pairs of springy brass contacts along the baseboard faces. This is cheap, simple— the connections in track wiring are made by contacts soldered to the rails—but has the defect that in permanent situations, dirt works its way down between the mating faces and spoils contact. This can be cured by rubbing with a nail file, but this is tedious and apt to cause damage.

when there is a break, or merely if you wish to alter the connections at the end.

SWITCHES

The control of a layout usually involves the use of a number of switches of various types. The divisions are first, function, second, type.

The functions concern, first the number of throws—or in the case of rotary switches, 'ways'. These describe the number of positions the switch can be set. In general toggle switches come as single throw, double throw and double throw with centre off, rotary switches are normally from 2- to 12-way, though rotaries of 16-, 20- or 24-way types are occasionally encountered.

Next there are the number of poles involved. In the case of the toggle switch, this is normally one or two, but rotary switches can have a very large number of poles, but obviously, the more poles and throws, the greater the cost. It is possible to get a DIY rotary switch, where one assembles the required number of wafers onto the switch body.

Although for the most part one pur-

On the whole, the cost of multi-pin plugs should be faced.

Some simplification is possible where, instead of taking all the wiring onto the nearest baseboard to the control panel, the panel has a series of cables connecting directly to each section.

There is no one basic system that is best. Most developed layouts tend to use a multiplicity of approaches developed on a pragmatic basis. Indeed, when one is working with multi-pin connections there is a great deal to be said for employing a variety of types, for when only one pattern is used, it is only too easy to put the wrong plug into the wrong socket.

TEST EQUIPMENT

For most model railway purposes the main test needed is that of continuity. It is interesting to find that there are plenty of ways of doing this.

The simple light tester, battery powered, shown in the diagram, is the most obvious. Replace the light with a buzzer for an audible check.

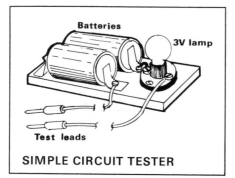

Batteries

3V lamp

Test leads

SIMPLE CIRCUIT TESTER

For checking the supply of current, a lamp on leads, rated at 12V, will do the trick nicely. A commercial version, using a 12V festoon lamp in a translucent plastic case, is available. More sophisticated devices using LED indicators, are coming into use because of their robust nature; test gear is commonly abused.

However, the most useful type of all-round test equipment is the multi-meter. For our use we do not require an ultra-sensitive, accurate device, the main criterion is the provision of DC and AC voltage and DC current readings, plus a measurement of resistance.

In general the current measurement facility is of little value, since the range is too low for our use. The resistance measurement is invaluable for continuity tests, for although we are seeking zero resistance, the meter will indicate a low resistance in a badly made circuit in addition to the nil reading for an open circuit. Voltage readings, taken across the track, will tell if current is getting through.

To increase the versatility of test meters and circuit testers, a couple of leads with crocodile clips at each end should be acquired. These can be used to bridge gaps, or to connect one test probe permanently in circuit whilst checking a number of circuits.

POWER UNITS

I have left consideration of power supplies until last for the simple reason that all units from reputable manufacturers are perfectly satisfactory in their major function, to supply a controllable electrical feed to the layout. There is the con-

Airfix MTC command control.

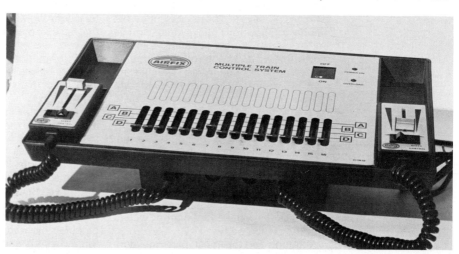

Hammant &
Morgan HM3000
electronic
controller.

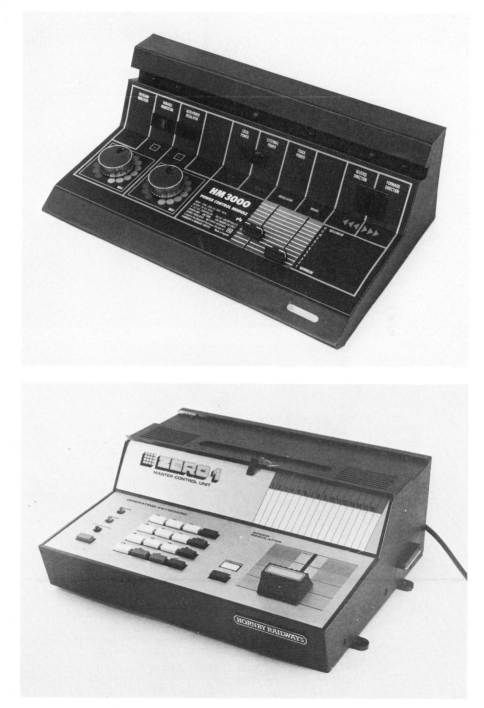

Hornby Zero 1
Command Control
Unit.

sideration that the less you pay, the lower the power output.

There are two basic divisions, straight and electronic. At one time electronic controllers tended to have almost as many knobs as a hi-fi rig, but of late the designers have come to realise that a model railway operator has only one hand, so far as the controller is concerned, the other is needed to work the point levers and switches, and, whereas, to continue the analogy the hi-fi buff has ample time to balance the controls, the railway operator must be able to make instantaneous adjustments.

As a result, present moves in elec-

Compspeed
'Rambler'
controller.

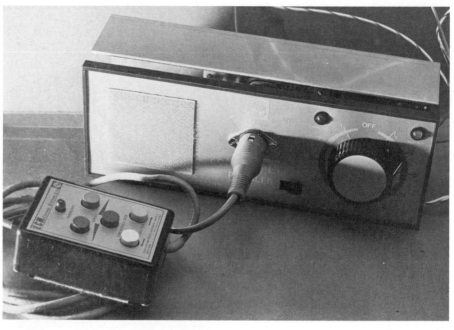

Close-up of
Rambler hand-held
controller.

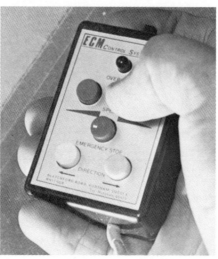

tronics are making good use of solid state capabilities to sort out the finer features automatically and to make the locomotive run at the desired speed in the desired direction which is, after all, the object of the exercise.

One advantage of an electronic controller is its ability to be miniaturised, making it particularly suited for small panel mounting modules or even hand held control units.

Leaving aside the simple units contained in many train sets today—most of which are only just adequate for their work—the standard resistance unit consists of a large metal or plastic case,

with an integral transformer and a single, or in the case of twin output units, a pair of knobs. A separate 16V AC supply for auxiliaries independent of the DC supply is usually incorporated.

Whilst some electronic controllers have a built-in power source, more and more require an independent 16V AC supply. As a result they are much lighter, the relatively heavy transformer can be placed securely on the floor.

Possibly the best known, certainly the most reliable manufacturer of combined power units is Hammant & Morgan, they have recently produced a rather elaborate transistorised unit, as well as a command control system completely compatible with the Hornby Zero 1. The units are built to the full requirements of modern safety regulations and, providing (as with all other mains powered equipment) the plug is correctly fitted, they are absolutely safe. The major train manufacturers also provide power units, but such is the predominance of H&M as an efficient brand leader that over some fifteen years no-one has been able to make a dent in their market.

The more specialised manufacturers, wisely, have concentrated on the transistorised unit. Here the fall out has been fairly rapid, but several firms seem to have become established.

At present ECM seem to have established a solid following with their Compspeed module. This is a single-knob

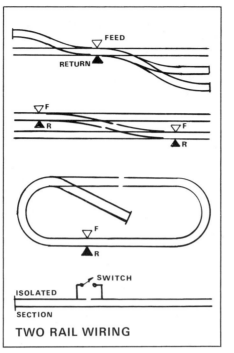

Feeds made at toe-end of points.

Breaks between pairs of back-to-back points.

Breaks in all continuous runs.

Isolating sections have a break in one rail bridged by an an-off switch.

FEED

RETURN

F

R

F

R

F

R

SWITCH

ISOLATED

SECTION

TWO RAIL WIRING

POWER REQUIREMENTS

The normal OO gauge locomotive requires about $\frac{1}{2}$ to $\frac{3}{4}$ amp at full power, most units will just about supply enough power to run two locos at once. Except where this is done for special effect—usually for double-heading—it is not a good idea.

Allow roughly 1 A clear per train, and keep auxiliaries separate. Point motor supply should be separate from lighting.

The paradox of a well developed layout is that the power requirements of the trains are well below those of the auxiliaries, but even so, do not even begin to approach that of the lighting.

WIRING THEORY

In this essentially practical book, there is no space to do more than touch briefly on the basic theory of model railway electrification. It should, at the outset, be made clear that there is nothing inherently difficult about it, the apparent complexity arises solely because there are so many circuits involved.

TWO RAIL WIRING

At one time it was considered that two rail wiring practice was extraordinarily difficult, but when the schoolchild with his, or her train set succeeds, why should the adult worry?

The following rules explain what has to be done. Little more is needed, and the exceptions only occur in specialised situations. The more straightforward layouts are easily wired in this manner.

1 Take two wires from the power unit to the length of track from which the turnouts radiate. On large layouts several feed points will be needed.

2 You *must* put insulation gaps in each rail where turnouts are back-to-back. Additionally there must always be at least one pair of insulation gaps in any continuous run.

3 Term one wire 'feed' and the other 'return'. Any section switches must be in the feed wire; it is advisable to take all feeds independently to the control panel or unit, but all returns can be linked in common.

4 To isolate small sections, i.e. in loco sidings, platform roads etc., place insulated joiners in the feed rail. Bridge the gap thus formed with a pair of wires leading to an on-off switch or a push button.

module, with a most useful feature, it measures the back emf from the loco motor and adjusts the power feed accordingly to keep the speed constant. Not only will it keep a train running at constant speed up and down gradients, but, an even more severe test, it has persuaded a locomotive with a set of binding side rods to run smoothly instead of progressing in cyclic jerks.

The Compspeed is now obtainable as the 'Rambler' where a small push-button unit, the size of a matchbox, provided with five buttons, enables the operator to control his model purely by touch. Furthermore, the unit, which has a 5-DIN plug connection, can be detached and plugged in elsewhere on the layout while the train is running. This provides 'walk-around control', generally regarded as the most convenient way of running a model railway, since the operator is not fixed to one position, a boon on all but the smallest of systems.

COMMON RETURN

Where each controller has a completely separate supply—in other words, does not take its power from one transformer secondary output—it is possible to keep all returns common. This has several advantages and few disadvantages, and for this reason, it is to be preferred.

Wiring with DPDT switch.

Wiring with two controllers.

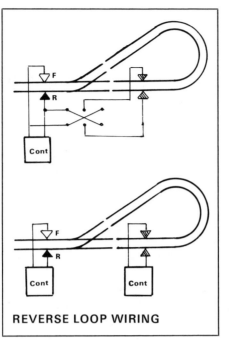

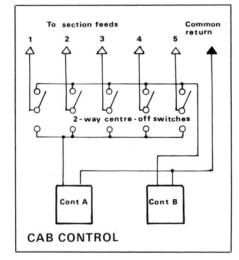

REVERSE LOOP WIRING

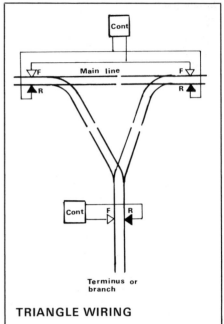

TRIANGLE WIRING

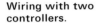

CAB CONTROL

REVERSE LOOPS AND TRIANGLES

On reverse loops and triangles we get the situation where the left hand rail meets the right hand rail and, if nothing were done, a short circuit would result. There are several ways round this impasse.

The simplest, and most elegant, is to avoid the use of reverse loops and triangles in the first place. It is worth pointing out that the majority of good, successful model railways do not include them, indeed, in practice, they are only of much value on a very large system indeed.

If you must, there are two practical solutions. The first is to completely isolate both ends of the loop and to feed the isolated section through a reverse switch. Although this is generally fed from the controller, and as a result the train has to stop, if the loop section is fed from a second, auxiliary control, taking its supply directly from either a 12V DC output on the main controller, or from a separate power supply.

In the case of a triangle, it is usually arranged for a terminus to feed a continuous main line. In this instance, the best solution is to have one controller on the main line and another working the terminus. Both controllers have to be set in unison in order to pass a train across the gap.

CAB CONTROLLER

The normal arrangement for a double track main line with a set of independent sidings is to have three controllers, one for the up, one for the down line and one for the yard. It frequently happens that to get a train into the yard, all three controllers are involved.

It is possible to arrange switchgear so that, for such a shunting move within station limits, the yard control takes precedence, the other two being switched out. This is an elementary form of cab control, elementary, that is, in terms of

The old 16-switch bomb-release control (now, sadly almost unobtainable) makes an excellent switchboard.

flexibility but if, as is sometimes the case, the switchgear is combined with the lever frame working the points and signals so that the changeover occurs automatically when the roads are set for a shunt, then the arrangement is quite sophisticated and really, beyond the scope of this book.

A simpler arrangement is to divide the entire layout into blocks and to arrange to feed these from any controller. There are many ways of doing this, but British practice tends to favour the use of a selector panel.

If we assume two controllers, then if each block has a three-way switch which can be set to either of the two controllers then you can easily set up routes for each operator. The ex GPO Key switch is so ideally suited for this purpose, having three positions and more than enough contacts to do the work. Indeed there are enough to allow anyone with that turn of mind to add a range of colour indicator lights to the model control panel. While this would be superfluous if all controllers are on the main panel—the purpose of the switches serves the same purpose, it would be useful where two of the three controllers

are separated, since the operators would then know exactly where they could run.

Alternatively, multi-way rotary switches can be employed. These are easier to obtain than the ex GPO equipment, which tends to turn up unpredictably in surplus stores.

COMMAND CONTROL

In recent years a new system of control, which requires a module to be fitted in the locomotive to decode the instructions transmitted from a complex controller has been developed. Known as 'command control', it appears to eliminate a great deal of wiring, using the rails to carry both traction current and instructions not only to the locomotives, but, in certain recent systems, points and signals as well.

Furthermore, a lot of emphasis has been placed on the ability of these systems to allow one to control two trains independently on one circuit of track. This is not their true purpose, for in practice, unless both trains travel in the same direction at the same speed they collide. They give an improved form of cab control, for each locomotive will only move on command and will remain put, anywhere on the entire system, when you want it to. It should, perhaps be stressed that in all forms of model railway control, the problem is not so much of getting the locomotive to move, but rather of arranging matters so that it does not move when you do not wish it.

In essence the system involves fitting every locomotive with a module—often called 'the chip'—which receives signals from the controller and only responds when its specific channel is energised. The system is not new, but the British system has two important features in common. It will handle 16 locomotives apiece, which is slightly more than any overseas rival, and, more important, the chips are the smallest so far produced and the only ones capable of being fitted into the great majority of steam outline locomotives.

Command control possesses many inherent advantages, but it does have the snag that every locomotive has to be fitted with a module. The cost is likely to be high, and one immediately loses the advantage that a locomotive can be purchased and put straight into service. Paradoxically, it seems to be most effective on relatively small, simple systems, where the greater flexibility of operation consequent on the ability to hold any locomotive stationary anywhere on the layout, shows to its maximum advantage. On ultra-portable systems, the facility for operating points and signals with only

Behind a panel using semi-rotary switches. Note the use of tag strip.

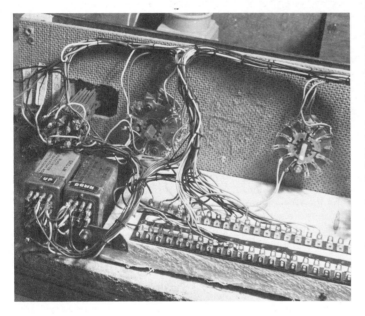

Fleischmann relays for automatic control and block sectionalising. These can be used with any make of equipment.

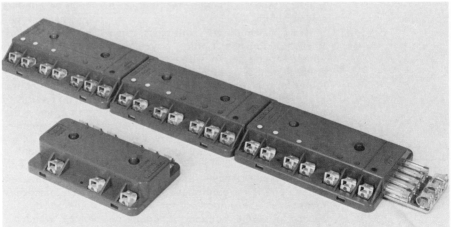

two wires from the control panel to the layout, and just two connections between each baseboard is again a useful side benefit.

CONTROL PANELS

Many layouts seen at exhibitions have control panels which look like a cross between an electric organ and a fruit machine, with overtones of NASA Mission Control. The reason is that somewhere in the club there is an electrical fanatic with a weakness for SF films and TV, whose hobby is really the construction of complex control panels.

The simple fact is that anyone can easily give an excuse for incorporating a mass of meters, indicator lights and batteries of switches. At least half of them serve only to provide information the operator can more readily obtain by looking at the layout. Indeed, it is a sound principle that if the operator can see what is happening, there is no purpose in providing indicators to tell him so all over again.

The fact is that a very simple control panel is perfectly adequate. There are two preferred patterns. The geographic panel, with a diagram of the layout and switches on the sections they control is simple, easily understood and has only one serious disadvantage, any alteration to the layouts involves a reconstruction of the panel.

The alternative has the switches in a simple regular bank, numbered. A diagram showing which switch does what, in the form of a prototypical signal box diagram is provided.

Both systems closely parallel full size

railway practice. A third, very sophisticated system begins by having the layout not only correctly designed, but fully signalled. It is then controlled by a correct pattern signal lever frame, with switchgear arranged to energise only those tracks set up. There are no switches, realism is high, but because of its complexity, the layout design is effectively frozen. Therefore, only advanced modellers, using a prototype station plan, should consider it.

AUTOMATIC CONTROL

The easiest way for an absolute beginner to get into deep water is to try to design a system of automatic control.

There are several excellent Continental systems on the market which can provide this facility. Although designed for use with specific branded makes, in practice, once the principles have been grasped, they can be employed on any system. ECM manufacture a very sophisticated system which gives automatic retardation and acceleration.

It is not, in my estimation, a good idea to get deeply involved in automatic control at the outset. The simple fact is that all automatic systems take over from the operator, and furthermore, at present, have very limited capabilities. It is possible that, within the next decade, the microprocessor may provide the answer at not too high a price. Unfortunately, to date most of the attempts have reached the point where one begins to wonder if the railway itself is not redundant, a minicomputer, a couple of taped programmes and a VDU would enable one to simulate the operations of any chosen main line. But this would be home computing, not model railways as we understand them.

Landscape & Terrain

THE PROBLEM

In creating a realistic model landscape, one is faced with the difficult task of reproducing the infinite variety of nature. Here your own individual artistic skill is brought into play, and for this reason alone, the modeller should carefully examine his abilities before venturing too far on an ambitious scheme. There are ways round the problem that will suit those with little or no artistic bent. As with all things, one should studiously avoid trouble and not set out to demonstrate to everyone your inabilities in any specific field.

Terrain comes in a variety of categories, ranging from the gentle undulating low- lands to near vertical rock walls. This is only the start, for the railway must cut through the natural slopes of the land. It is rare indeed for anything more than a simple roadside tramway or an inexpensive light railway to lie directly on the actual ground, even rarer for there to be a level piece of ground of any size. The railway line is carried on embankments through cuttings with bridges, viaducts and tunnels.

Cutting and embankment sides have a very definite slope, set by the nature of the soil. Where the angle of repose—as this slope is termed—is very low, toe walls are provided to reduce the amount of space needed. Full height retaining walls are only adopted where land costs are

Elaborate scenery on an American style HO layout.

Showing a typical
cutting and
embankment.

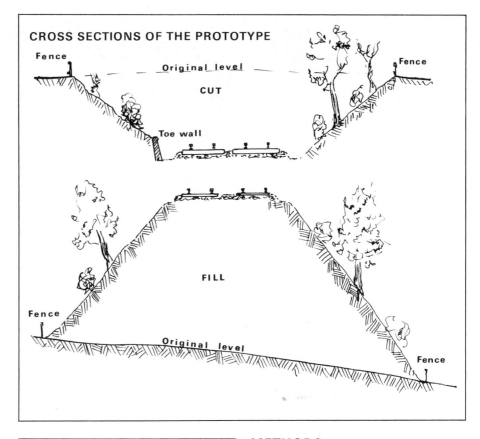

CROSS SECTIONS OF THE PROTOTYPE

Fence

Original level

CUT

Toe wall

Fence

FILL

Fence

Original level

Fence

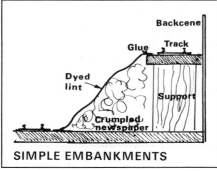

Backcene

Glue

Track

Dyed
lint

Support

Crumpled
newspaper

SIMPLE EMBANKMENTS

very high or, in certain cases where a later line has to lie close to an existing railway.

It is very rare on a model to have sufficient room for a true angle of repose to be modelled; it is permissible to introduce a slightly steeper slope to save space.

It should be noted that the man-made slopes are normally uniform, the even nature of the sides is only affected by a need to introduce some lineside structure or where a landslip has occurred—for engineers have been known to mis-calculate the angle of repose on many occasions.

METHODS

There are nearly as many methods of modelling terrain as there are experienced landscape modellers! The simple fact is that all methods work, some are limited in scope and best applied to only a specific number of applications. Only a handful can be used for every situation, and even so one needs a fair degree of skill to be uniformly successful. The main point for the beginner to keep clearly in mind is that despite the confident statements of acknowledged experts, all of whom claim that only their method is truly reliable, *they all work.*

In this field, more than any other, the individual's skill is of prime importance, some people are able to manage certain techniques better than others. The moral is to try everything until you hit upon one which works for you.

We will now look at the basic methods.

THE MAT

Once upon a time, green fields were made from old green chenille table-covers! It wasn't very realistic, but it is the genesis of the scenic mat.

Scenic mats are available from commercial sources. Some, alas, are just grotty, others, more expensive, are very good. Used judiciously, they can give an excellent effect if one accepts the fact that the colours are, in general, too bright.

All commercial scenic mats tend to be stiff and are not suited for anything more dramatic than a gently undulating ground surface. Indeed, one rather feels the makers expect the majority of users to lay them directly onto a flat surface, which might suffice for a bowling green — a sports stadium is perhaps too large in this context. Always slip a little packing under the mat to get the humps, hollows and hillocks.

A home made scenic mat is both cheap and fairly versatile, the basic materials is medical lint. This can be dyed, for you neither want a uniform hue or the adventurous patterns created by tie-dying, just a general mishmash graduating from one colour to another.

The lint is then stuck down over a substrata of crumpled newspaper. Fortunately, grass, in its natural form, tends to bulge over road surfaces, and so the edge of the lint can be made to look remarkably realistic.

A slightly better, and rather faster system using lint has been developed by Peter Denny. The lint is first fixed in position with the fluffy side up, then coated with size, then, whilst the size is still wet, painted with poster colours. The advantage of this system is that the size stiffens the lint and the ground surface is firm.

All mat systems work well for grassy surfaces. They are relatively clean and free from mess, and are ideally suited for work in the living area of the house.

SOLID LANDSCAPE

It has always, in theory, been possible to have a landscape carved from a solid lump. The snag has always been the weight and work involved. Expanded polystyrene sheet solved this particular difficulty.

This sheet can be obtained in bulk in thickness up to several inches. It is not very cheap, bought for the purpose.

It is extensively used in packaging, and, in thinner sections, is sold as ceiling tiles. Often, decorators offer cheap seconds, these are ideal for our purpose, but in practice, not the most useful, because the lowest priced supply of expanded polystyrene is in packaging throw-outs.

It is lightweight and remarkably firm when properly treated. However it can only be effectively cut by the hot wire technique. It isn't difficult to make a hot-wire cutter, and anyone aiming at extensive use of expanded polystyrene sheet should manufacture one. For carving the material, a simple spade bit fitted to the end of an electric soldering iron, or even riveted to a spare bit, will carve surplus expanded polystyrene from the mass.

It is, of course, absolutely essential only to use the special cement sold for fixing ceiling tiles, and furthermore, it is vital to check all paints used on the material since many paint solvents attack the material.

It should also be stressed that expanded polystyrene is excessively flammable.

PAPER SHELL

There is one simple, low cost technique for landscape surface, the paper shell. The principal material is newsprint, which in the majority of households tends to build up at an alarming rate. On the whole the serious broadsheets, notably the *Telegraph* and *Guardian*, are marginally better than the *Sun* or the *Mirror* because they tend to use a slightly better paper. On the other hand, page 3 of the *Sun* could provide some interesting relief.

The other essential ingredient is wall-paper paste. The only point to note here is that because we are working in a more restricted area, under no circumstances

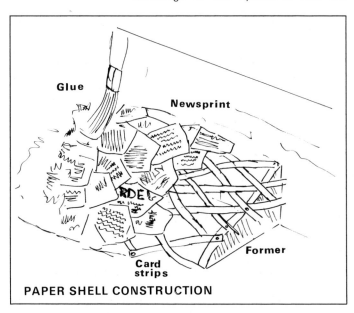

Glue

Newsprint

Former

Card strips

PAPER SHELL CONSTRUCTION

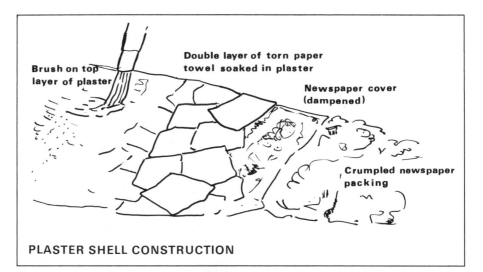

PLASTER SHELL CONSTRUCTION

Brush on top layer of plaster

Double layer of torn paper towel soaked in plaster

Newspaper cover (dampened)

Crumpled newspaper packing

Foundation of newspaper for plaster shell.

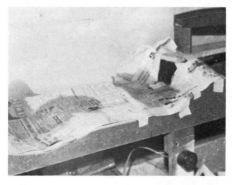

Plaster shell terrain before texturing.

follow the instructions and mix up a bucketful. An old cup or jamjar is ideal. A little experiment soon shows the correct proportions of water to powder, store the balance in a screw top jar.

Whilst this system is usually carried out over a sub-frame, it is not difficult to work on a crumpled newspaper foundation, It isn't generally realised that one can stick large sheets of newspaper over quite large gaps with the aid of any sticky tape, or even staples from a staple gun. Extra large gaps are best covered with grocery bags. Don't worry if they sag.

On top of this sheet, build up the con-tours on the landscape with crumpled balls of newspaper. You'll find it best to stick them in position with paste, or hold them down with a strategic piece of tape.

Now cover this rough formation with sheets of newspaper, slightly dampened to make them conform to the sub surface. Push it around, stick flaps down until you arrive at your desired formation.

Now tear a sheet of newsprint into pieces about 2 in in length. Don't try to get them all square, it just doesn't matter. Apply wallpaper paste, using a scrap of board for the purpose, and press them lightly in position onto the framework. Carry on until the whole surface is covered. It may be just possible to apply a second layer, but avoid getting the whole area so soggy that the newsprint tears under its own weight. Now leave to harden. This will take at least 24 hours.

Apply a second coat, let this harden, then a third and possibly a fourth. Leave the final coat, which will bring the shell up to around 1 mm in thickness, to harden for a week, then remove and discard the crumpled newspaper and its support from underneath. The end pro-duct is a light, rigid and, except in time, inexpensive ground surface. Further-more, it can be cut with a sharp knife if you want to remove any portion.

PLASTER SHELL

A rather faster landscaping method uses hard casting plaster and paper towels in place of the pasted newsprint. With this method the hard shell is formed over-night, and in general, only one layer is needed. Up to now the problem has been

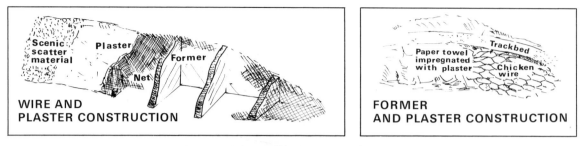

WIRE AND PLASTER CONSTRUCTION

FORMER AND PLASTER CONSTRUCTION

A variety of scenic development can be seen in this photograph, rock face to the front, grass slope in the far left, and, to the right, cut out trees and hills to create the back scene.

obtaining hard casting plaster, at least in conveniently small quantities—50 kg bags are all very well, but when 5 kg is ample for most purposes, they come rather expensive. However, the recently introduced Linkalite casting powder is ideal for this form of landscaping.

The plaster is mixed to about the consistency of pancake batter, using a flat dish. The paper towels are torn into pieces about 2 in long and as wide, flipped in and over so they are coated—visit your local fish fryers to study the technique—and applied over the paper foundations described above. Leave to harden, then remove the crumpled paper support.

WIRE AND PLASTER

An old technique, still greatly favoured, involves spreading plaster over fine chicken-wire. Alternatively, you can use expanded aluminium, if your bank balance is healthy enough.

The favoured plaster is the normal filler, of which Polyfilla is so well known as to have become the generic term. Avoid plaster of Paris or Keans cement like the plague, they harden too rapidly.

The plaster needs to be stiff enough not to fall through the holes in the wire mesh, and has to be spread with a small trowel. It is a very messy method, which, one suspects, is the main reason for its popularity. The plaster shell tends to be thick, since it becomes essential to apply a thinner finishing coat over the top of the base coat, which is difficult to smooth properly at the first attempt.

PLASTER AND FORMERS

One can, instead of chickenwire, build a landscape over a series of profiles. These are occasionally miscalled 'contours' but as every schoolchild should know, contours lie flat, not in the vertical plane.

The formers can be cut from anything you have to hand. They will be hidden anyway.

Over the formers you pin strips of thin card, criss cross, to form a rough landscape. Next you cover this with thin material and finally coat it with plaster.

This method is recommended by Jack Kine, who built many models for the BBC TV and certainly creates magnificent results. He also supplies a special scenic plaster which is smooth, stiff and, above all, stays workable if kept in a screwtop jar for a very considerable time indeed. This method is, one feels, best suited for the more meticulous modeller working in a relatively restricted area, but, except for the expert, would be excessively time consuming if applied over really large spaces.

PLASTER BANDAGE

It is possible to use the plaster impregnated bandage used in hospitals to immobilise broken limbs and the like. This is sold under the trade name Modrock. To use, it is soaked in water and spread over a former. It is relatively simple, not unduly messy but of necessity, rather more expensive than most other systems.

OTHER METHODS

There are several other methods that have been employed to produce terrain. Most are fairly costly. One however, is cheap, true papier maché. (The paper shell system is occasionally miscalled papier maché), but this system involves mixing paper and size into a gooey mess in a bucket. This process takes quite a while. Then the resulting goo is spread over the scenery. Its main fault is an inordinate drying time, over a week. The paper shell system is to be preferred.

Various plastics, ranging from the obvious fibreglass to a range of proprietary two-part foam mixes have been proposed. They work after a fashion, but cost the earth. We're only supposed to be modelling it. Forget them.

SURFACE TEXTURE

With the sole exception of the scenic mats, all these terrain systems produce a featureless surface lacking in texture. There are various ways of remedying this.

However, before we begin, certain surfaces tend to end up a little rough. A

Rock faces can be carved in plaster. Apply mix to at least $\frac{3}{16}$ in thick, and begin roughing out before the plaster is hard, in careful hands, this is very realistic.

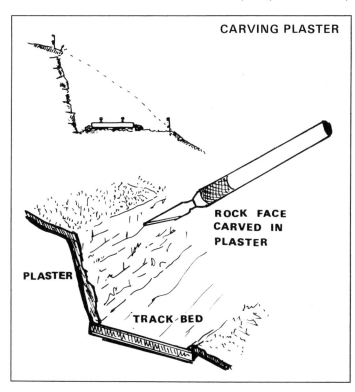

CARVING PLASTER

ROCK FACE CARVED IN PLASTER

PLASTER

TRACK BED

thin plaster coat cures this, it is best applied with a cheap flat paintbrush, around $\frac{3}{4}$ in wide for convenience.

The commonest surface texture is produced by a scenic scatter material. It is stuck down with oil-based paint rather than glue, this enables you to colour the ground surface the appropriate colour, which should be matched to the actual area you intend modelling.

Scenic scatter materials are very mixed. A lot are coarse dyed sawdust, and look what they are. Some are much finer and should be preferred. If you want to produce your own (and there is a very good reason for this; commercial colours tend to be rather too garish), try to get hold of some hardwood sawdust from a cabinetmaker rather than the coarser stuff from your local woodyard. If you have a sawbench, then you will probably produce all you need, the smaller home sawbench generally produces very fine dust.

You can use dye, or oil based paint, let down with white spirit. Put the colourant in a glass jar, add sawdust until the colourant is completely soaked up, then spread over a metal tray to dry. Use the domestic oven after a baking session, or arrange trays over a radiator to speed the process.

It is a good idea, after covering the painted surface with scatter material, to press it firmly down, using a paper kitchen towel laid flat over the texture.

As an alternative, sand can be spread

ZIP TEXTURING

(labels in figure: Tap gently!; Mixture of powder colour & plaster; Fine sieve; Texture falls naturally on terrain; Dampened plaster base)

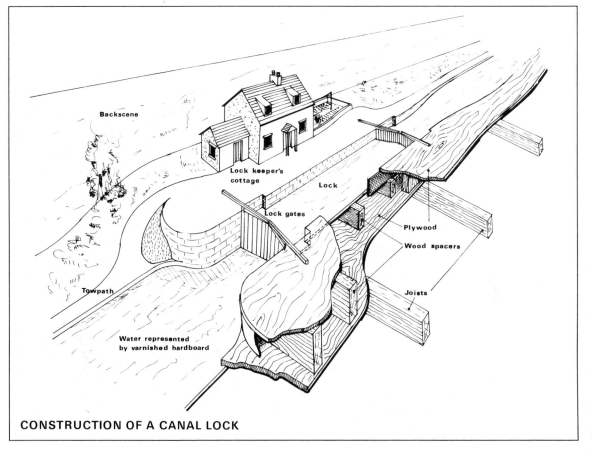

CONSTRUCTION OF A CANAL LOCK

(labels in figure: Backscene; Lock keeper's cottage; Lock; Lock gates; Plywood; Wood spacers; Joists; Towpath; Water represented by varnished hardboard)

over the surface. Here, glue is preferred, PVA adhesive, diluted about 10-20% with water is ideal. After the sand is dry, the surface is painted. For this, an airbrush is best.

Indeed, the airbrush is an invaluable tool for improving the texture of model landscape. It applies paint finely, without disturbing the surface, and is an ideal method of graduating the colour. In general, an airbrush capable of taking a cup as well as a jar is best for this type of work since one needs to change colours fairly often.

Whether you paint the surface or merely use pre-coloured scatter materials, there are two important rules to remember. The first is that natural colours are subdued, and, moreover, you are not modelling the colours in close up, but at a distance. Many otherwise excellent models are marred because the ground is too garish. The second is that uniform colour is very rare indeed. The sole exception is a high class lawn, a day or so after mowing when the banding effect has worn off.

ZIP TEXTURING

A neat and effective method of producing a quick and effective surface texture is to mix plaster of Paris with pure powder colour. This mixture is then dropped from a small sieve onto plaster which has been dampened with water. To persuade the powder to drop, tap the edge of the sieve (a plastic tea-strainer is ideal) with an old spoon or something similar.

The plaster of Paris combines with the powder colour to produce a fine textured surface. Various colours can be blended, and since the texture is put in place by gravity, as on the prototype, it looks right. The plaster also serves to let down the hues of the powder colour.

COLOURING

It is impossible, in a purely verbal description to explain exactly how to colour landscape. The most important point is to avoid garish colours. Even in sub-tropical zones the effect at a distance is muted, in temperate zones, colours are soft.

Avoid pure black and only in chalk areas, permit the pure white of the plaster to show. Aim at the warmer tones, use a good colour guidebook of your chosen locale as a master, remembering that there is generally a tendency to exaggerate the intensity of colour in such publications. If you are not aiming at any specific area, select your colours from your own locality.

WATER

The trouble with water is that it is, if anything, more varied than the ground itself. It is however, not unduly difficult to reproduce in model form, providing you know what you intend to reproduce in the first instance.

Let's begin with the simplest method, still, dark water, the sort you find in canals and docks. You need for this flat surface, this is where hardboard really comes into its own. Paint it dark brown, with or without a bluish tint. Then coat with varnish, and protect it from dust whilst drying. The result is at worst a reasonable representation of still water, running deep.

By streaking the brownish blue ground with bluish white and then applying layers of varnish with thick brush strokes, the effect of slow moving water can be achieved. However, Murphy's Law ensures that, whereas when you wish to varnish a door, let alone a piece of furniture, you always get brush strokes, when you want them to appear, it is more difficult to arrange it.

At one time an effective way of creating the effect of running water in small streams was to use crumpled cellophane, stretched out between the banks. The problem today is finding cellophane, plastic sheet has largely replaced it. About the only place it is still used is in florists, so while you could try to track down their source of supply, a more elegant solution is to buy your wife/girl friend/mother a bouquet, which will additionally, sweeten the atmosphere.

Now we come to the more complex methods. Instead of a flat surface, we model the bed. From here, there are two approaches.

One uses a piece of transparent plastic to represent the surface of the water. In skilled hands this can be lightly streaked with paint, have weeds and small debris put on the surface and, finally, ripples painted on the top with varnish. At the same time you can model rocks on the bed—use small washed pebbles and select the most evenly rounded ones. You can add miscellaneous debris. Small tufts of weed can be stuck into small drilled holes, indeed, quite a lot of things can go into close fitting holes in a plastic water surface. It is possible to include bathers if you are very careful. In such cases, a little cement can be used, or better still, a two part epoxy resin since this dries transparent.

CAST WATER

However, if you want to get a lot of debris half in and out of the water, then you must use other means. Varnish, and quite a few two-part self curing plastics dry more or less transparent, and can form very realistic water.

There is one important thing to remember. In such cases, it is vital that the bed of the stream, river or lake is absolutely waterproof, or you will find yourself

MODEL LAKE WITH PLASTIC 'WATER'

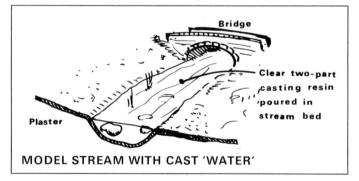

MODEL STREAM WITH CAST 'WATER'

pouring in a good litre of the goo, only to discover that ·9 litre is on the floor, congealing into a horrible mess. Another hazard is that varnishes not only take an inordinate time to dry in depth, because a skin forms on the surface and prevents further evaporation of the solvent, but they tend to shrink and crack whilst doing so. The best method with varnish is to apply successive thin layers to build up the depth. With this method a careful worker can give the effect of real depth by applying very thin, transparent washes of paint at varying levels. It is also possible to include model fish swimming in the water.

The two part plastics can be poured to the full depth at the outset, since their hardening is the result of a chemical reaction. But for their price, they would be the ideal way of representing water.

RUNNING WATER

So far we have been considering the more or less placid stream, river canal or lake. In upland country, rivulets are much more active and their successful representation calls for two considerations.

The first, fairly obvious condition is that the water has to be represented either by varnish or cold setting plastic. Since young streams are generally fairly shallow do not add any colourant to the mix, let the bed, which will generally be of water-washed gravel, show through clearly.

The second condition is more subtle. Water does not flow uphill. It is however, very easy when modelling a watercourse to introduce a small upgrade which, forever after, looks subtly wrong.

The way to avoid this is to pour a trickle of real water down the dry bed beforehand. This will reveal the natural flow of your watercourse, you make a note and then put your varnish or plastic where the water went. Naturally, you have a basin at the bottom to catch the overflow.

It is even possible to erode a water-

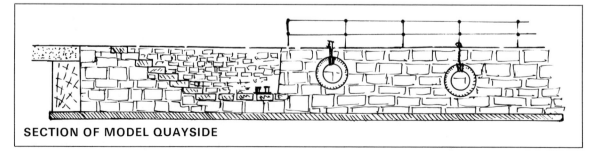

SECTION OF MODEL QUAYSIDE

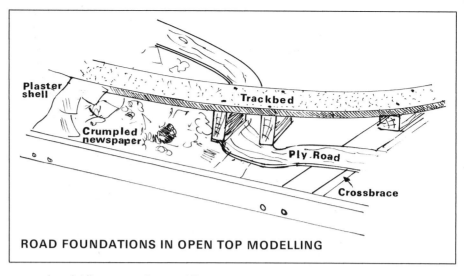

ROAD FOUNDATIONS IN OPEN TOP MODELLING

course by trickling water down whilst the final plaster coat is still soft. You can't get much nearer to nature than that.

HOW NOT TO DO IT!

There are two ways not to model water. The first is to use real water, it is out of scale. It is just permissible if you must have moving ships on a very large model, but the size needed for this is such that it is, in the main, best left to the larger exhibition model. The second is the use of ripple glass. It doesn't look very effective, it is heavy and, above all, it is very easily broken. One model railway with a glass canal had to have a narrowboat run into the bank lying diagonally across the 'water' in a most unusual fashion solely to hide the crack.

We could add a third. Mirrors do not look in the least like water, for all that they are sometimes used in toy farmyards.

Having mentioned cracks, it can occur that an extensive river scheme is too big for any available sheet of plastic. The solution here is to arrange the inevitable joins underneath low bridges.

One final word, if you want water in the landscape, in many ways a canal is the ideal solution. A set of locks not only makes an effective model, they introduce the all important change of levels.

ROADS

Compared with water, roads are extremely simple. The main surface is made from hardboard or stiff card. Since few roads, other than major motorways and expressways are absolutely level, packing must be used to produce gentle undulations.

Fortunately, few road surfaces are higher than their immediate surroundings, even when on an embankment, so it is possible to pin the road surface down along the sides and then hide the pins under the verges. A fine plaster screed can be added if desired but it isn't always necessary. Any motorist knows that a road surface without the occasional repaired trench across its entire width is highly unusual, thanks to the amiable habit of the utility services waiting until the highways department have resurfaced that section before renewing their mains! Such a trench can be used to disguise the inevitable joints in the road surface.

A quick way to create the grey of asphalt is to paint black and sprinkle with scouring powder whilst still wet. Brand new asphalt can be reproduced by sticking 'wet & dry' abrasive paper to the surface.

It is extremely difficult to paint accurate road markings in small scales, and since nothing looks more toylike than badly painted road markings, leave them off. If you must, very careful masking, and the use of precision cut templates, in conjunction with an airbrush is probably the best solution. You will go slowly crazy trying to line a long stretch of model road.

Cats-eyes, on the other hand, are relatively easy to simulate. Obtain a selection of brilliants from a craft shop and cement them into drilled holes in the road surface. They aren't correct, but, like the prototype, they catch the light, and the eye.

It is important, on period models, to

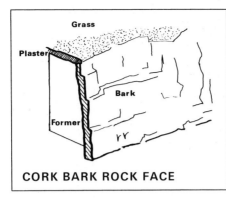

CORK BARK ROCK FACE

found to have interesting strata. It is superior to natural rock because it is decidedly lighter.

Some experts take moulds from actual rocks, using self curing latex rubber, then cast rocks in plaster. This is really only a sound practice if you have a large area to cover, for then it is possible to make a number of different moulds and thus vary the texture.

The ultimate is to carve the strata in the plaster surface. Oddly enough this is not quite so time consuming as it might seem, particularly if you begin roughing out before the plaster has hardened.

remember that present-day roads differ considerably from those of the 1930's, the road signs in particular are radically different. In pre-group days, tarmac was rare, pre 1900 it was virtually unknown.

ROCK FACES

Rock faces are not too difficult to model effectively, for there are a number of simple methods. The easiest is to crumple a piece of aluminium kitchen foil, open it out and apply this to the wet plaster surface. Allow to harden and peel off the foil.

Almost as simple is the use of bark, though to many this expedient looks remarkable like bark at all times.

Limestone outcrops can be modelled by splitting pieces of softboard and arranging them as strata. If you are in an area where you can burn coal, the occasional lump of slate (or, not so occasional as the case may be) may be

MESS

Most landscape modelling methods involve a good deal of mess, one way or another. In point of fact, plaster brushes out of cloth and carpets with only a little extra effort, but it does seem that there is something in the female psyche that cannot be reassured, even by practical demonstration. So, only bachelors living alone should attempt scenic work without taking a few reasonable precautions.

First, spread a protective cover over the floor. A stout polythene sheet is probably best for this, though an old sheet will be less bother. Next, wear old clothes. Finally—and this is for your own comfort, have a bucket of clean, hot water on hand. It won't stay hot, but it won't end up freezing either. You use it to wash plaster, glue and the like off your hands from time to time. Naturally, an old, but serviceable towel will be needed as well.

Bridges & Tunnels

Bridges and similar civil engineering structures are not exactly part of the landscape, but they play an important part in creating the overall scenic picture. The following notes must of necessity be very general, and at all times a careful study of the prototype is required. It is as well, in this context, to point out that there is no such thing as a 'company' design of bridge, or for that matter, of any specific civil engineering structure, they are, in the main, functional items, if there is any evidence of ownership it is generally in the form of applied cast iron decoration. There are some obvious exceptions, Brunel's fan viaducts were distinctively Great Western (or to be exact, distinctive of companies in the GWR sphere of influence) but most of the more obvious examples are large, distinctive, famous structures which have no peers. The Forth Bridge is a case in point, it is unique.

KITS

An excellent selection of kits for bridges and viaducts exist. Most are of Continental origin, but here there is no particular nationality in such structures. It is more a question of whether they fit the requirements of the situation.

The majority of girder trusses are best modelled using kits although there is absolutely no reason why such a structure should not be scratchbuilt, other than the sheer magnitude of the task. Probably the best material to use is Slaters Plasticard Microstrip, which is not too difficult to

These attractive bridges were made from commercial plastic kits.

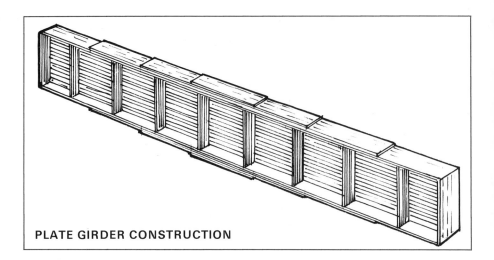

PLATE GIRDER CONSTRUCTION

(Below) Plate girder bridge made from card.

A light girder bridge, built from odd bits of plastic kits, with wire handrails and embossed plastic card abutments.

PLATE GIRDER BRIDGES

The simple plate girder is normally scratch-built for the simple reason that it is far and away the most straightforward form of bridge one can devise. Again, plastic card is the best material for this purpose, and the degree of elaboration involved depends partly on your own perseverance and, equally important, on the location of the girder on the model. It is not really worthwhile putting every bracing girder and angle plate on a model which is well away from the viewer. The diagram shows the simplest form.

It is relatively simple to proportion a plate girder so it looks right, the rule of thumb formula is that the depth of the girder in inches is twice the span in feet, a ratio of 6:1.

MASONRY BRIDGES

A masonry bridge is a more challenging model, again the diagram shows a sound method of construction. In all masonry structures, the arch is vital. It is not true to say that the keystone holds the whole in place, it is just the last part to go into the structure. The arch can be a true arc, an ellipse, or the pointed 'Tudor' style, which was used by Brunel at the Bristol end of the GWR, and by other engineers when they could get away with it. It is vital to look at actual prototypes and study their proportions.

In general, stone bridges are older structures, after about 1880 brick became the normal material. The exceptions occur where, in the 20th century, aesthetic considerations in an area with good supplies of stone suggested that the

fabricate into angle, T channel and I section girders, while gusset plates can be cut out of plastic card, as can the webs and flanges of the larger structural sections. Providing you copy a prototype (or have the knowledge to design a girder bridge for yourself) the resulting structure will be extraordinarily strong.

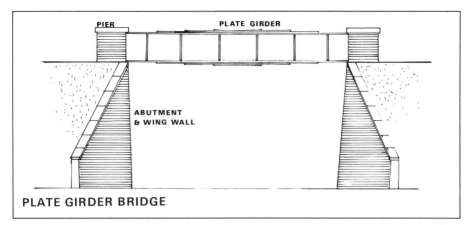

PLATE GIRDER BRIDGE

A 3 arch masonry bridge with the 'Tudor' form of pointed arch. Note refuges over abutments.

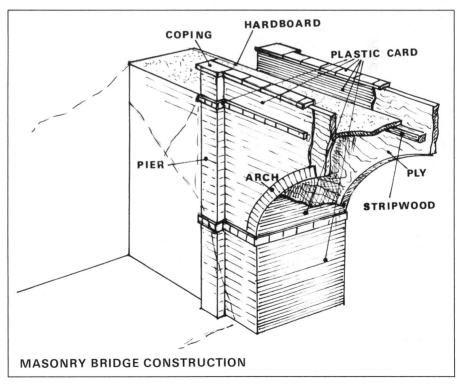

MASONRY BRIDGE CONSTRUCTION

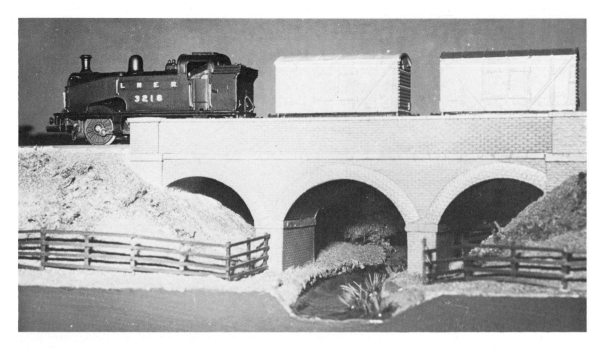

A typical 3 arch masonry bridge in 3 mm scale. Note the brick arches.

abutments of girder bridges should be in this material.

CONCRETE BRIDGES

Most recent bridges are made from concrete, mostly pre-stressed girders. On electrified lines, odd hybrids, older abutments carrying an odd shaped concrete raft across the tracks appear where clearances had to be increased to give sufficient air gap for the 25 kV lines.

Concrete is easy to model. One simple method is to cut the girders from close grained wood with a fretsaw. The grain has to be filled and sanded smooth before painting. Today, plastic is preferred. Although plastic card might seem the obvious answer, in point of fact the solidity of a concrete girder is often easier to portray with perspex sheet, painted in

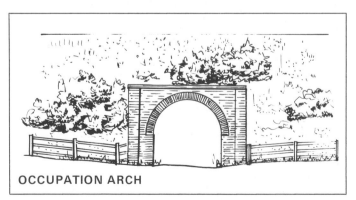

OCCUPATION ARCH

the appropriate colours. Again, study prototypes. Unfortunately, most of the more exciting concrete bridges span motorways, not only are they inappropriate for our prototype, but they are virtually impossible to study without risk of prosecution.

ACCOMMODATION BRIDGES AND CULVERTS

Where railways cut through farms or estates, access must be maintained. Whilst, wherever possible this is done by means of an accommodation crossing, which makes an excellent model; embankments are pierced by accommodation arches. These are frequently quite low structures, possibly no more than

PIPE CULVERT

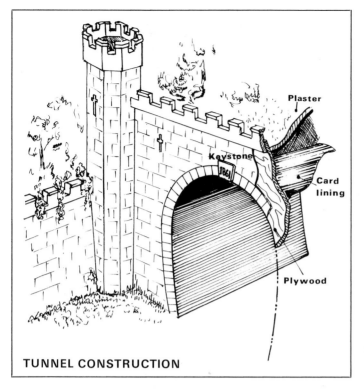

TUNNEL CONSTRUCTION

(labels: Plaster, Keystone, Card lining, Plywood, 1861)

This elaborate tunnel mouth is one of the pair of Lorelie tunnels produced in kit form by Faller.

crete or brick invert to the top of the arch. In recent construction, or reconstruction, concrete pipes are employed instead. Indeed, when the Liskeard bypass was built across the Looe branch in Cornwall, the railway was carried through in a large concrete pipe.

Where access is needed across a cutting, a glorified footbridge is provided. Not infrequently, it was a timber structure to save expense.

TUNNEL MOUTHS

At first sight a tunnel mouth can be regarded as nothing more than a bridge facade, but there are differences. Except for a few relatively recent cases, where circular cast-iron tubes have been driven through suitable ground, (normally on electrified lines) tunnels have an elliptical section.

Much more to the point, this section should give ample clearance above the loading gauge in order to prevent smoke accumulating at the level of the footplate. Some bores were tight, and in steam days were sheer purgatory for the enginemen.

Tunnel facades were frequently embellished. The reason for this is obscure, for few are in a position where they can be seen, it was not until the advent of the diesel multiple unit train that passengers could enjoy views along the line. However, it does allow the modeller to indulge himself by adding turrets and battlements to taste.

RETAINING WALLS

Where land is expensive, retaining walls are employed to support the sides of a cutting. A few were masonry, some recent examples are either mass concrete or concrete block, but the overwhelming majority of British retaining walls are made of brick, frequently the hard blue engineering brick which, it is reputed, will outlive the Pyramids.

It is very unusual to find a perfectly plain brick retaining wall, largely because the flexibility of the medium at a time when highly skilled bricklayers were plentiful, hard working and not exactly overpaid for their efforts, it was possible to reduce the quantity of brickwork by judicious use of piers and relieving arches. None of which, needless to say, exactly simplifies their representation!

Since a brick retaining wall makes a very effective, neutral backdrop to a

seven feet to the top of the arch, and would, in general, have patches of worn earth or mud on either side, unless the owner had prudently laid down several loads of hardcore. Small streams are carried through in culverts, these are usually even smaller low tunnels, often only four or five feet from the constation area, and moreover, can bring a row of housebacks or shop fronts high above the train roofs, and thus prevent them being hidden from view, it is well worth taking a little effort. The Linka system of plaster casting can be adapted to produce retaining walls with a little ingenuity. The more elaborate retaining walls provide a distinct challenge to the modeller with sufficient patience and determination to tackle the intricacies involved.

REFUGES

Wherever clearances beside the line are limited, refuges must be provided at regular intervals so that permanent way staff can get clear of passing trains. They take the form of small projections outward over piers of viaducts, recesses in narrow cuttings and small arched cubbyholes in retaining walls with insufficient depth behind the piers to give safety. They are also to be found in tunnels, but here it is not practicable to show them in model form unless, purely for the sake of effect, one models a half-cut away tunnelled section.

WALLS AND FENCES

Boundaries, from time out of memory, have been marked by some permanent division, for even a notional marking defines the extent of one's territory and helps avoid inadvertent arguments. When railways came, Parliament decreed these dangerous devices must be firmly fenced.

For the main the post- and rail-fence was preferred, though later the post and wire became more popular as it was

RETAINING WALL DETAILS

T1 4-4-0 passes over a bridge on H M Pyrke's 00 gauge Berrow branch.

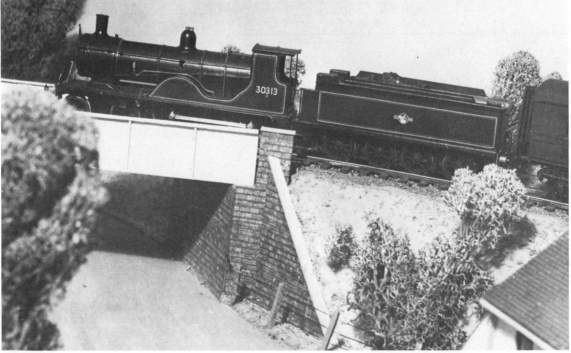

realised that most people kept off railways, and the minority were not deterred by the most formidable obstacle. It was not until the advent of electrification that it was felt necessary to make the boundary more secure.

Walls were less common, except where there was ample stone, and enough men available who understood the art of drystone walling. Brick walls are in the main, urban arrangements.

The fencing at stations is more elaborate. Close paling fencing is normal, but often one will find iron palings. These last, in model form, can be soldered from wire on a simple jig, but of late some beautiful brass etchings have come onto the market.

Where fences follow contours, the upright posts are just that. Of the proprietary post and rail fences, only the excellent Peco product will do this readily. With other versions it is more work to make it conform than it is to scratchbuild the fence from plastic strip.

On slopes, brick walls move upward in steps, the brick courses at all times being level. Only a drystone wall follows the lie of the land.

TREES

Although commercial trees are available, they are in the main either unrealistic or expensive. Some are both!

A common fault is lack of height. Most mature trees are higher than a house, it is only the specially bred ornamental species that are relatively low. This means that it might be a good idea to omit trees were it not for the fact that, outside the purely urban areas, trees are common sights along the boundary lines of all British railways—except, of course, in areas where no trees will grow anyway.

A good way of modelling a tree is to take a bunch of soft iron stranded wires, bind them together with parcel tape and then fan out the wires to form branches.

Post and rail and vertical iron paling fences are prominent on this period 4 mm scale model by Mike Sharman.

TREES

Trees add considerably to the effect of the landscape and are well worth taking some trouble to make. The best foundation is a wire trunk and branches, with foliage added. Teased out scouring pad and fine scatter material are now the preferred materials, but dried dyed used tea leaves have been used with effect.

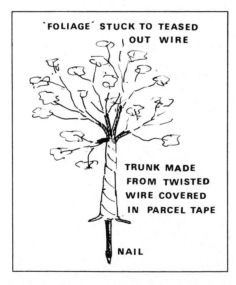

'FOLIAGE' STUCK TO TEASED OUT WIRE

TRUNK MADE FROM TWISTED WIRE COVERED IN PARCEL TAPE

NAIL

Foliage teased from scouring pads and embellished by scatter material can produce a most realistic model. There are textbooks which give the correct shape, height and foliage for every British species.

Oddly enough, once the technique is mastered, the production of realistic model trees is not too difficult, and is an ideal fireside (or should one nowadays say TV side?) occupation. Moreover, these trees will not succumb to Dutch Elm Disease.

A rather quicker method is to select suitable twigs, or better still, suitable root systems from plants one removed from the garden, and garnish with dyed lichen. The result, whilst not so effective, is reasonably quick. It is particularly useful where it is desired to model a copse or small wood. It would also work for a forest, if such a model were a practicable proposition.

HEDGES AND SHRUBS

Hedges can be made from lumps of dyed lichen arranged in rows, or, if you can obtain it, from rubberised horsehair, once the basic material for upholstery. It makes, when painted, an excellent representation of a quickthorn hedge.

Buildings

Pubs are favourite prototypes! (Below) The 'Wheatsheaf' is on H M Pyrke's Berrow Branch. (Bottom left) An English pub kit by Pola. (Bottom right) Heljan's kit for a British pub.

On a model railway buildings can be divided into three categories, railway buildings proper, private buildings on or adjacent to railway property connected with the railway's business and finally the rest. The first category is essential if the model is to look right, the second category is advisable to round out the picture and the third group is used to give some sort of justification for the railway.

This point needs to be made, for all too often newcomers, excited by one of the layouts which are heavily embellished with realistic looking buildings, are apt to consider that unless there is a village close to hand the model is lacking. Be warned, the latest, and most effective model in this particular genre has so little railway that even the owner considers it is a bit of a problem to find it!

CARD KITS

There are, today, plenty of kits available for the modeller. Most British railway building kits are made from printed card. Some of these, designed for quick, effective assembly, are perhaps a little lacking in subtlety and need very careful work if they are to look their best. The old Superquick kits, which have been unaltered for something like fifteen years, are pre-cut from stout card and in general make up well. The Prototype building kits are, as their name suggests, based on actual, identifiable railway structures, they are probably the most difficult to make well, insofar as the builder has to cut the parts out for himself, but the effort is well worthwhile. In recent years the range has been improved by the addition of plastic parts which replace certain card fittings that were difficult to assemble cleanly.

Town scene
from Vollmer Kits.

A busy scene
produced from
Faller kits.

PLASTIC KITS

Plastic building kits for the British scene are not so plentiful, though two Continental manufacturers, Heljan and Pola, through their British distributors, Hales and Kohnstam (Riko) are beginning to make an impact here. Hornby have begun to introduce some plastic kits alongside their ready built structures, which, whilst toylike in conception, are capable with a little work, of filling a gap on the layout, since they are well proportioned and follow the traditional 'Railway Gothic' style. Ratio are producing some effective railway structures.

The great mass of Continental building kits are such excellent models of their prototypes that a fair proportion would look a little out of place in a purely British scene. However, industrial buildings translate with very little difficulty, and a careful selection among the many types available can produce some surprisingly effective Anglicised models. Many of the modern houses and bungalows would look very effective if fitted into a typically English garden setting of recent times.

However, if one is prepared to do more

(Top left) Plaster station building kit by Osset Mouldings.

(Top right) A corner of a Vollmer display. Note the careful use of figures.

(Above) A wintry setting, using plastic building kits.

than just a little cosmetic treatment, most plastic kits can be successfully adapted in ways their designers probably never conceived. In many ways, the Pola range of industrial structures, which has a strong common bond though a standard pattern brick walling and substantially similar doors and windows, are ideally suited for cross kitting. Some very impressive large industrial buildings have been created from these.

Before we move on to the question of scratchbuilding, mention must be made of the new series of small buildings and accessories produced by Wills Finecast. These are mainly of structures that are to

be found in the immediate vicinity of a station, and are self coloured and easily assembled.

SCRATCHBUILDING

The absence of a myriad of suitable kits should not be regarded as a great tragedy, for it is in this field where scratchbuilding really comes into its own. Whilst a fair proportion of all towns and cities is given over to repetitive spec built and council housing, it is only on absolutely new developments that individuality doesn't creep in. Around most railway stations there is a welter of different buildings, sometimes in the penultimate stages of decay, sometimes in prime condition. As a result, the modeller's individuality can have full rein.

The traditional medium for building construction is card and wood, but of late plastic card has begun to take a larger slice of the field, a process accelerated by the advent of embossed plastic sheets representing brick, stone, tile, etc.

Plastic card has several advantages. Of these, undoubtedly the most important is the ease of working. It is slightly brittle, so the method of cutting is to score the surface with a craft knife, then snap off the part cleanly. Internal openings are usually made by scoring diagonal cuts from corner to corner and then pushing out the unwanted parts. A little experiment is needed to get the hang of the technique, but it is if anything, easier than normal cutting out, certainly in the thicker grades.

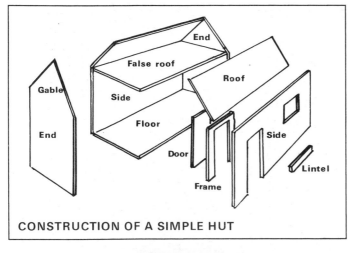

CONSTRUCTION OF A SIMPLE HUT

Plastic card can also be drilled and sawn, while the edges can be finished off with a file, an emery board or on sandpaper laid flat on a level surface.

Once cut, plastic card is readily joined by one of the many plastic solvents on the market. Slaters Mek-pak is the general favourite. It is not excessively toxic, but it is very flammable, for this reason it is not a good idea to store large quantities indoors. The manufacturers will supply bulk quantities in screw-top metal cans for safety, pour into small screw top bottles for general use.

Plastic solvents are applied to the jointing faces after the parts have been put together, they flow through the joint by capillary action and produce a firm

Wood and card kit for a windmill by Marlow Models.

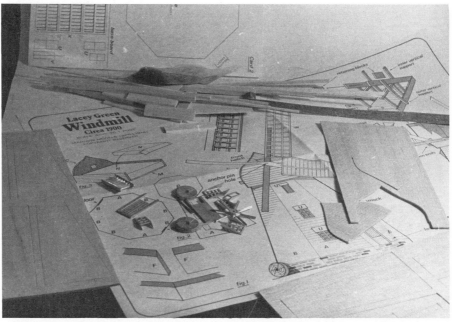

A complex building in 3 mm scale, made from embossed plastic sheet.

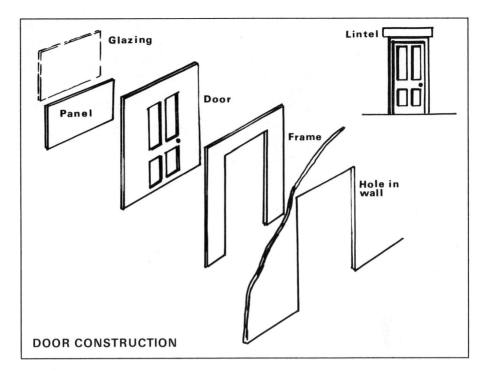

DOOR CONSTRUCTION

(labels: Glazing, Panel, Door, Frame, Hole in wall, Lintel)

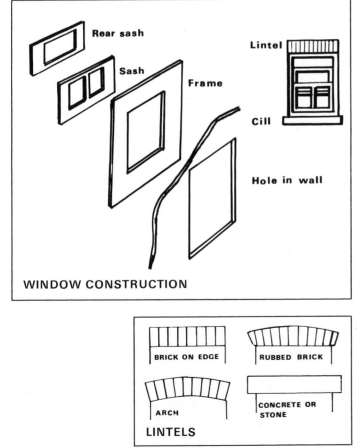

WINDOW CONSTRUCTION

(labels: Rear sash, Sash, Frame, Hole in wall, Lintel, Cill)

BRICK ON EDGE   RUBBED BRICK

ARCH   CONCRETE OR STONE

LINTELS

weld. Furthermore, although it takes several hours for this weld to harden thoroughly, it is usually strong enough to hold together after around 15 seconds, and firm enough within one minute to take the strains of adding further parts. Plastic cement may also be used with plastic card, but it does take much longer to harden. Finally, plastic card takes paint well, and needs no surface filling.

BUILDING CONSTRUCTION

If you remember the old song about modern housing estates, it referred to 'little boxes made of ticky tacky'. Substitute plastic for ticky tacky and you have the idea. All houses are a series of interlocking boxes, some flat topped, some with slopes at the top.

Probably the best thing to begin with is a simple hut, just four walls, a door, a window and a roof. Description is tedious, a sketch shows the arrangement. From here, it is not too difficult to work one's way up to more elaborate structures. With plastic card, plain or embossed, construction is straightforward.

Because the embossed sheet is fairly thin, 20 thou in point of fact, it can either be applied to a thicker sheet as a sandwich and allowed to harden overnight under weights, or it can be fully braced behind.

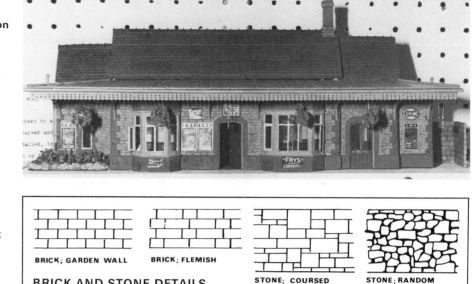

Scratchbuilt 4mm scale model of Brimscombe Station building by W Baker.

Roofs are most in view on a model, it is well worth adding extra details, such as dormer windows, fanlights etc.

BRICK AND STONE DETAILS

BRICK; GARDEN WALL   BRICK; FLEMISH   STONE; COURSED   STONE; RANDOM

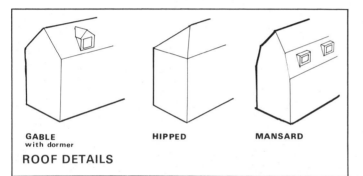

GABLE
with dormer

HIPPED

MANSARD

ROOF DETAILS

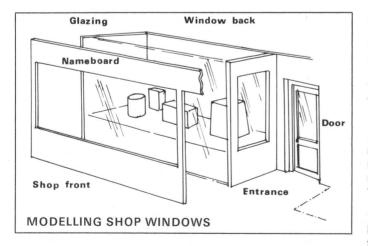

Glazing   Window back

Nameboard

Door

Shop front   Entrance

MODELLING SHOP WINDOWS

The art of miniature building construction is a fascinating one. Anyone setting out to explore this field should study not merely his local buildings, but also obtain a few illustrated books on architecture.

SHOP FRONTS

Shops make very popular models, they have considerable interest to the viewer and provide a challenge to the modeller's ingenuity.

The large sheets of plate glass are readily modelled from thick transparent polystyrene. This is easier to locate than you might think, there are many display boxes made from this useful material nowadays, these can be cut carefully with a medium pitch saw. Clear polystyrene sheet is extremely brittle and is even easier to shatter than glass. It is probably best to make a transparent box and then add the fascia in the form of overlays of 20 thou sheet platic card.

The fun in window modelling is providing the stock in trade. This is not too difficult, given a little ingenuity. There is however one very important point to bear in mind, the transformation of the High Street in recent years. Any steam-age scene calls for a lot of care and not a little research, whilst the pre-nationalisation scene is full of pitfalls. Remember, that television did not spread outside the London area until the very end of the 1940s and wasn't nationwide until the late '50s. Most modern signwriting stems from the design impetus given by the Festival of Britain and therefore pre-nationalisation scenic work needs careful study of old photographs.

Luckily, there are more and more albums of old photographs being pub-

Model shop fronts from kits. Simple printed scenes provide a reasonable amount of detail, but for full realism one should model the merchandise in the round.

Low relief structure from wood, card and brickpaper.

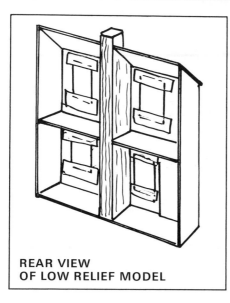

**REAR VIEW
OF LOW RELIEF MODEL**

lished nowadays. These certainly assist in the business of making a model scene more authentic.

LOW RELIEF

To model a street in full detail takes up a great deal of depth, something which, on the average model railway is in decided short supply. The appearance of a town behind the railway can be suggested by modelling a series of low relief buildings along the backscene.

The low relief building is no more than a facade. Strictly speaking, it isn't always this, if one models a row of house backs, or the rear or side of a factory or warehouse in this fashion, technically speaking you are not showing the facade. Possibly the idea sprang up from the film set, where only the bit facing the cameras is finished,

A pleasing array of scratchbuilt structures around a level crossing.

An industrial corner of H M Pryke's Berrow Branch.

A fine 4mm scale signal cabin.

behind there is an array of struts and braces holding it all together.

The second great virtue of low relief modelling, after the obvious one of space saving is that one is only modelling the interesting bits, the dull work is omitted in its entirety. As a result low relief structures tend to be more detailed.

It is a good idea, when modelling a row of low relief structures, to vary the styles, heights and, where the situation warrants it, the depth and even the alignment of the facades. Of course, there is no reason why you shouldn't model a fine Regency terrace if that is what you like. Unfortunately, fine Regency terraces and railway lines are not commonly found in close proximity one to the other! There is always, of course, our old friend, modeller's licence.

LINKA

There is one method of producing buildings, walls and other features made from stone or brick which, whilst strictly speaking, a scratchbuilding approach, is still strongly akin to kit construction. It is the Linka system of cast plaster construction.

The basis of the Linka system is really quite old, brick or stone walls are cast in plaster. The essential difference is that the unique plastic moulds are very well made, the sections are cast in modules complete with a comb pattern joint edge, to a basic modular size. Some sections have windows and doors cast in them, others

An impressive station complex made from Linka castings.

are plain. Still further sections are provided with arches. In addition to the brick and stonework walling, there are tiles and even wood sections provided.

Equally important, each set comes complete with a mixing bowl and measures for plaster and water, ensuring that the consistency of the mix is always right. Further accessories cast round towers, stone sets, plain sections for floors or flat roofs. There is nothing that cannot be made from Linka, with a little ingenuity.

The over-riding advantage of plaster walling is that, when painted with a thin wash, the colour sinks into the porous material in a highly realistic fashion. It has often been employed by commercial firms to produce models, but the inherent disadvantage is that it is heavy and brittle and accordingly, like some wines, does not travel well. However, when you cast-it-yourself these difficulties disappear.

Probably the only initial snag with Linka is that one has to cast the units some hours—or better still, days—before one begins building. This can be a trifle

frustrating, but once you've built up a stock of parts, then creating a complete original building is a positive pleasure. It's a good idea to collect a lot of those plastic pots margarine and some butters come in these days, they make ideal storage units for the various parts for, obviously, it isn't a very good idea to put them all in one large container and then scrabble around to find the one you want.

The cast walls are very even, as is right and proper. Older buildings usually have a few bricks showing signs of spalling—losing their top faces. A little judicious work with a fine pointed craftknife will take care of this. Stonework is often quite uneven at the outset, so get cracking with the knife.

We said you could complete an original building quite quickly. Well, it doesn't have to be original. Although the modular nature of Linka makes it a matter of coincidence that one could make an exact scale model, given a good photograph and commonsense replica of many prototype structures.

Locomotives & Rolling Stock

Most railway modellers begin by purchasing ready-to-run locomotives. This is a sound policy at any time, now there are so many excellent, well detailed models on the market, it is rather ridiculous not to take full advantage of the glut.

DIESELS

Although there are, at the time of writing, a few British main line diesel locomotives not available in a completely finished form, the omissions are not serious. There are kits, but in general they fall short of the quality of the ready made versions, and are more costly. The diesel fan follows prototype practise and purchases his requirements from a specialist builder.

He does not stop there. As bought, the models are much too clean, and, since one usually needs at least two of each class, there is the business of re-numbering and possibly adding a new nameplate. Brake and heating hoses and cables can

be added to the bufferbeams, front ends can be altered, as on the prototype. Sundry other small changes can effectively customise the model.

STEAM

Most r-t-r steam locomotives are *much* too clean. This is particularly so in British Railways days, and in the immediate post war years of company ownership. In the 1930's principal express locomotives were generally kept clean, but freight locomotives were often mucky. Some were very mucky.

Handrails were rarely polished. They used to go rusty if this was tried.

KITS

The number of steam classes that existed in the 1950's, let alone at earlier times, was such that it is highly unlikely that more than a fraction can ever be supplied

Period GW locos run through a model of Dawlish station.

Scratchbuilt 7mm scale broad gauge models.

Mainline 'Western' class diesel hydraulic.

LMS Compound 4-4-0 by Airfix.

ready made. It is necessary, therefore, to supplement the range by means of kits.

Cast Whitemetal
The first locomotive kits were made from a soft whitemetal alloy, cast in rubber moulds. This certainly produces some intricate castings, but on occasions there is distortion and the fit is not all it might be.

Accordingly, loco kit construction is not altogether a simple matter. A great deal of fitting has to be carried out to ensure that that the parts go together snugly, and since soft lead-based alloys clog files, this can create some difficulties.

Ex Cambrian 2-4-0T kit by GEM with, (Below), the chassis out of the body.

acting two part contact adhesives seem to have definite potential.

However, many prefer low melt solder. Providing one uses a 12V soldering iron run at 10V, and employs a phosphoric acid flux, there is no undue difficulty. One great virtue of low melt solder is that it makes a superb filler for even large joints.

Most kit manufacturers can supply this useful material, usually in small packs sufficient for one locomotive. However some modellers have switched to Cerro-bend, an alloy with a melting point below 100°C, used primarily for bending small bore tubing in hydraulic plant. It is also used by some loco builders as ballast but is none too easy to obtain and is fairly expensive. (So for that matter, is low melt solder.) The advantages of Cerrobend are that the difference in melting point between the solder and the base metal is even greater, and furthermore, should something go wrong, it is quite easy to reduce the kit to its component parts; immerse in boiling water.

Underside view of GEM 2-4-0T, showing pickup.

Whilst a bastard cut file will remove the worst, there are two methods of removing finer amounts of metal. One is to make use of manicure boards, which are efficient at clearing whitemetal until they clog, but being quite cheap, may be readily thrown away. The second is to use small scrapers. These can be ground from old needle files and, if kept sharp with the help of a fine oilstone slip, will pare away surplus metal with ease.

The assembly of whitemetal kits can be carried out with adhesives or low melting point solder. Today, epoxy resins are favoured, but the recently introduced fast

Etched brass

A small but growing number of loco-motive kits are now being made from brass, etched not only to provide relief, but to shape the components. This type of kit will normally, given a little attention on the part of the builder, make up into a good model, whilst in the hands of an expert, the results are superb.

The main fault with the majority of such kits is that the instructions are far from detailed, in the main the case is that if you can put the kit together anyway, fine, if you've never built a loco beforehand you can have a three dimensional jigsaw puzzle on your hands. In one case (the

A whitemetal loco kit displayed.

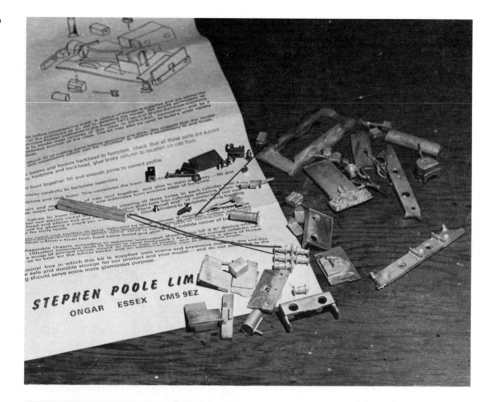

(Right) ECM motor.

(Far right) Sagami Can Motor.

K's HP2M motor.

A selection of worm reduction gears.

manufacturer has now ceased production), after a little while he lost patience and ended up 'Put the rest together in any order you think fit.' Whilst this was a fair statement, it didn't exactly help give the builder confidence.

This apart, these kits are in general excellent, since the detail is accurate and crisp, there is no suggestion of heaviness and the end result reaches the standards of the very best scratchbuilt models.

Assembly is by soft soldering, a certain number of whitemetal castings are generally incorporated. Most such kits make some provision for variants within the class; since in essence, an etched kit consists of accurately cut scratchbuilding parts it is not unduly difficult for a skilled modelmaker to carry out very extensive modifications.

Assembling a cast white metal locomotive kit. The kit as received, shrink wrapped on a display card. Instruction sheet on left.

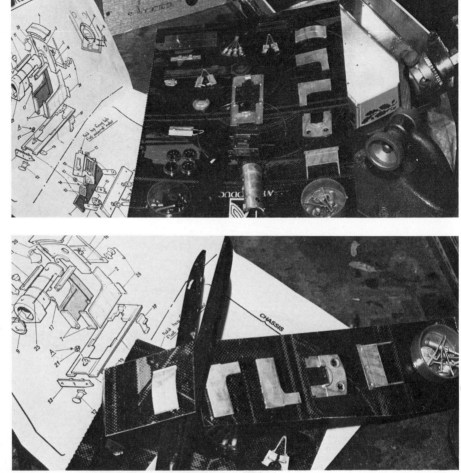

Cutting the card into pieces. Parts are left wrapped until needed; less chance of loss.

First step towards assembly of the chassis. The sideframes have been bushed, one wheel is on its axle.

SCRATCHBUILDING

It must be admitted that in 4 mm scale at all events, scratchbuilding locomotives is, today, very much a matter of eccentricity rather than necessity. Indeed, such is the impact of the r-t-r model and the kit that the majority of scratchbuilders have moved back into the 1890's or earlier to have a virgin field. Even so, this is none too safe, for the GWR, at present the most popular prototype, already has several 1890's kits and the move to broad gauge is no great help, for here a few kits are emerging.

Furthermore, the days when anything scratchbuilt was automatically good have vanished. In order to scratchbuild effectively one must be able to match the better kits, and this not only calls for a good deal of sheer determination, it also requires a fair amount of equipment. I say nothing of the skill involved, for given the desire

Chassis assembled (apart from coupling rods).

Underside view of completed chassis, showing arrangement of spring wire pickups.

to scratchbuild in the first instance, this can be acquired.

Since the craft of locomotive scratch-building has filled several books, all of which cover different aspects of the subject and, occasionally, to the new-comer appear to contradict one another (the explanation being that each author has his own methods) it is out of the question to do anything much about the matter in this book.

BITS AND PIECES

Although locomotive kits are well estab-lished, the supply of specialised loco-motive fittings has not disappeared, in-deed, after a lean period, it has developed. In many cases, the fittings have a wide sale among the kit bashers, who convert a kit for one class into another similar one by substituting fresh parts and adding a few odd items made in the home work-shop.

The most important fitting is undoubt-edly wheels, for, alas, many kits come without these all important accessories. Most people use either Romford or K's wheels, but the new Ultrascale range are growing in popularity as the range becomes extended.

Body assembly has begun. The main parts are set out, awaiting removal from the card.

Body and chassis awaiting final assembly. The chassis has already been tested.

After proving run, the finished model will then be painted.

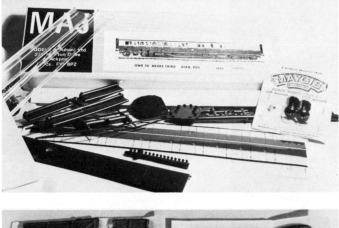

(Top) An MAJ 4mm scale coach kit. (Above) Plastic kits for 4mm scale narrow gauge stock by Dundas Models. (Right) Cast whitemetal locomotive oil lamps.

S. R. LOCOMOTIVE HEAD & TAIL LAMPS

The largest range of locomotive driving wheels is provided by Mike Sharman. He has one idiosyncracy, he only supplies direct at a limited number of exhibitions. This might seem an impertinence, were it not for the fact that the great majority of advanced workers not only attend these shows, but usually get their main supplies from Trade stands at shows. It is a simple fact that unless you happen to have an extremely good model shop on your doorstep, the best place to get your requirements is at a show. When buying specialised equipment, it is much more satisfactory to inspect before purchase.

The next important fitting is the etched nameplate. Most locomotive classes are now well represented and it is easy to fit any locomotive with a nameplate or numberplate where appropriate. It should be pointed out that only with an etched plate can one correctly represent this vital part of a locomotive's anatomy.

Boiler mountings and similar fittings are obtainable for most popular classes, whilst an array of bushes and other specialised parts can be bought. Again, this is something one can only get at the more well equipped shops, and again, at the major exhibitions.

ROLLING STOCK

It is very easy to think of coaches and wagons as something one hangs on the back of a locomotive in order to make up the numbers. In actual fact not only are there far more of them needed, but they come in many varieties. Into the bargain, they have to roll, which means that unless they run freely without falling off, there is trouble.

In practice most people start off by using ready built coaches and wagons. In general this makes good sense, for although there are many fine points to be observed in an advanced level project, one can get it off the ground that much sooner by using, as a stop gap, a selection of ready made stock. While, in the case of coaches and vans there are good reasons for making one's own stock, when it comes to open wagons and box vans particularly in 4mm scale and N gauge, the commercial product is extremely good for general purpose use.

WAGONS

In 4mm scale it is more and more the case that one builds from kits. Certainly, so far as freight stock is concerned, the selection of kits is such that one would be hard put to find a common, recent (i.e. post 1930) vehicle that is not available either ready to run or as a kit. Kits are available for selected pre-grouping vehicles, some dating back to the turn of the century. The standard British 4-wheel wagon has often been criticised for its stagnant design; this is arguable. What is definitely the case is that thanks to the longevity of design and the fact that, within the overall operating requirements and limitations, no remarkable progress could be made, ensures that, so far as the commoner vehicles are concerned, it is fairly easy to make models with a very wide application.

Furthermore, with the advent of the air-

4mm scale scratchbuilt Dean Goods.

(Below) Airfix GWR Centenary coach. (Middle) Mainline LMS corridor brake 3rd, (Bottom) Hornby MkIII buffet.

Three scratchbuilt PO wagons in 4mm scale.

Three Mainline PO vehicles.

Airfix container wagon.

Slaters O gauge cattle wagon kit.

something of a lottery. Without going too deeply into the subject, a PO wagon, in pre-war days, had a fairly fixed route and was not to be seen very far off of its basic area. This was the whole point of the exercise.

Exceptions were generally colliery owned wagons, and a few specialised hire firms such as Stephenson-Clarke (SC) — and oddly enough such vehicles are much rarer in model form than they were in reality.

Modelling a specific station in pre-war days (for the PO wagons were pooled in 1940 and working restrictions no longer applied), calls for specific PO wagons. It is unlikely that they will be available commercially, and so it is necessary to make one's own. Here the Letraset and similar rub-on lettering comes into its own.

VANS

Although vans appear to be a variation of goods stock, there was a separate sub-division of passenger rated stock. These were closed vans for valuable traffic which were fitted with running gear capable of fairly high speeds and continuous vacuum brakes. A limited selection is available in r-t-r form, several in plastic kits, but more and more are becoming available as etched brass kits. Not only does this stock give opportunities for interesting operation, but because it looks different, it tends to transform the layout on which it runs from the commonplace. It is probably the best field for initial construction.

brush and the current availability of comprehensive wagon transfer sheets, it is remarkably easy to finish a rake of wagons to a high degree of accuracy. The principal exception to this rule is the old private owner wagon.

The trouble here is that although both ready to run and kit PO wagons are available, the selection of names is

COACHES

In general, the core of r-t-r coaching stock is the ubiquitous BR standard stock. In a way this is misleading, since with three marks and three obvious sub-divisions in the Mk II stock, the choice is quite large. Furthermore, the oldest Mk I stock is rather less than fully covered in r-t-r and, since there are three basic types of bogie fitted to this stock, the opportunity for upgrading the stock exists. Finally, the gangwayed brake is not available in scale form.

However, moving to the steam era, the LMS is currently well supplied with the GW following close behind. One then moves into kits.

There are three basic types, plastic, combination and metal. The plastic kits are limited to two makes, Ratio and MAJ, the former need painting and concentrate on pre-group designs, the latter are pre-nationalisation and have pre-printed sides. They are possibly the simplest available and recommended for newcomers.

The PC coach is made from a variety of materials, it has a printed plastic sheet side and is rather tricky to assemble. The specification is continually being upgraded.

All metal coach kits fall into two separate types, punched sheet and etched brass. The latter are generally slightly more difficult to put together.

O GAUGE

Until the last couple of years, O gauge has been neglected by the Trade, but of late several small firms have entered into the field and are beginning to turn out some useful kits and components. We do not propose to particularise for the simple reason that in a relatively small field change is quite rapid. Suffice it to say that already there is enough to allow a fair start in the scale.

SCRATCHBUILDING

As in any area in this hobby, scratch-building is always an alternative, and since the essential components for rolling stock are beautifully standardised and not too difficult to acquire, the potential is considerable. Unfortunately to delve at all into the question would require another book so, since it appears that, at present, the ready availability of excellent kits has tended to reduce the amount of scratchbuilding anyway, I am glossing over this part of model railway construction.

Points & Signals

POINT OPERATION

There are three ways of operating a point, direct lever, mechanical remote and electric. Of the three, the simplest, cheapest and most effective is the direct lever.

(Top) Cycle spoke beneath baseboard. (Bottom) Wire-in-tube control.

(Bottom left) KTM point motor. (Bottom right) Ex government relays used as sub-baseboard point motors.

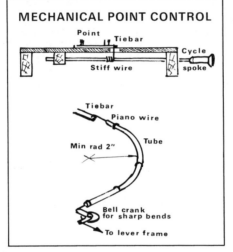

MECHANICAL POINT CONTROL

Providing, as is almost always the case, the point is within easy reach of the control position, it is simple to install and operate. It has one undeniable feature, it *always* works. For this reason it is to be preferred for the first attempts.

Next in simplicity is the electric point motor. It is not proposed to say over-much since every point motor is sold with full instructions, which should be followed. The main objection to this system is cost.

Mechanical remote systems are best suited to home construction. One very simple, very cheap arrangement calls for nothing more sophisticated than a cycle spoke, which, with the current upsurge of interest in what is probably the most cost effective form of short distance personal transport ever invented, should be quite easy to obtain. The cycle spoke slides under the baseboard in holes drilled in the baseboard sides and is connected to the point by a length of stiff wire which is coiled around the spoke and secured with epoxy resin. Whilst this does not give a centralised control position, the majority of well designed layouts have all principal turnouts within arm's reach to begin with.

For a centralised panel one needs a bank of levers and some means of con-

The distinctive starting signal gives character to Richard Chown's Irish broad gauge model.

Bracket signal worked by home-made electro-magnets.

nection. Believe it or not, the most obvious is still the most effective, strong thread, screw-eyes and a return spring. If absolute economy is the watchword then elastic bands will serve for the latter purpose.

Ratio produce a mechanical system. This was originally introduced for their ready assembled GW signals, but is now available in a variety of forms to suit any basic requirement. The only catch with mechanical systems is that they do not lend themselves to use on sectional layouts if a single lever frame is required. However, since it is often possible to split the frame across a baseboard joint, a very convenient arrangement is feasible.

For relatively low cost electric remote control, one turns to relays. The GPO 3000 type, with a gain stroke arm fixed to the armature, has been used to a considerable extent. Unfortunately, supplies of surplus relays are not so easy to come by (a brand new relay is quite costly) and so this system does depend very much on the availability of suitable equipment.

Relay operation also requires a supply of smooth DC current at 12V, if not 24V. This is something of a drawback for relative newcomers, but advanced workers regard it as a small price to pay for the two advantages of relay operation. The first is the fact that the contacts can be used not merely to provide positive energisation of the frog, but also for interlocking of power supplies. The second is that the control is by an on-off switch and

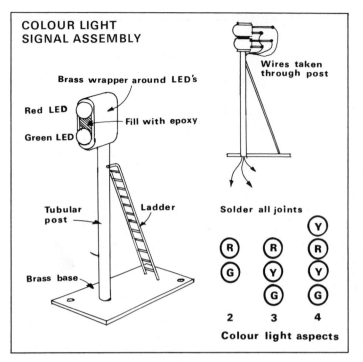

COLOUR LIGHT SIGNAL ASSEMBLY

Wires taken through post

Brass wrapper around LED's

Red LED

Green LED

Fill with epoxy

Tubular post

Ladder

Brass base

Solder all joints

2	3	4
		(Y)
(R)	(R)	(R)
(G)	(Y)	(Y)
	(G)	(G)

Colour light aspects

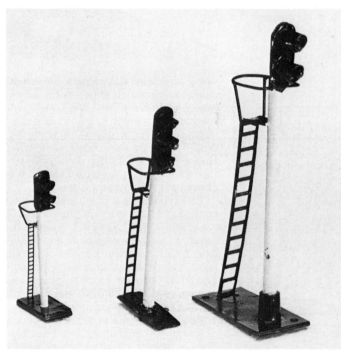

Commercial colour light signals for N, OO and O gauges.

unfortunately a fact that because in practice the driver, signalman and controller are one and the same individual, the layout will work perfectly well without them. As a result, signals are almost invariably the last item to be installed. The exceptions are those layouts where the owner is something of a signalling fanatic, in which case they are put in place quite early in the construction of the model.

There is one good reason for including signals, the design of the traditional semaphore is so distinctive that this, more than any other static factor, tells the knowledgeable viewer exactly which company's practice is being followed.

At present 4 mm scale is best served with signal kits. Ratio produce several kits which, with a little careful mixing and matching are capable of reproducing any modern (i.e. post 1925) semaphore installation. They also provide a range of fully assembled GWR signals and kits for 2 mm scale upper quadrant semaphores.

Still in 4 mm scale, there are etched brass components for the more exacting modeller. The largest range is provided by Derek Munday under the Sprat & Winkle brand. Advanced workers prefer metal signals, not only does etching provide somewhat better detail, but the metal parts are easier to make work—and when finished the signal is much stronger, which, in view of the fact that it is rather vulnerable, is a very good point.

COLOUR LIGHTS

The simplest type of signal to make fully operative is the modern colour light. It is also the easiest to model; the basic principles are shown in the diagram. Tiny grain of wheat bulbs can be used, but of late the LED is taking charge. This is not only on grounds of convenience, but on cost and robustness. Very small LED's are now available, and since the provision of a ballast resistor permits their use on 12V DC it is probable that they will be the colour lights of the immediate future. After all, their standard colours, red, green and amber, are those of colour light signalling.

SIGNAL OPERATION

In general colour light signals are either controlled by manual switches or by relays in a fully automatic configuration, much as on the full size system. Sema-

is accordingly much easier to incorporate into an automated control system.

SIGNALS

Whilst it is true to say that a model railway without signals lacks character, it is

Semaphore signal operated by home-made solenoid.

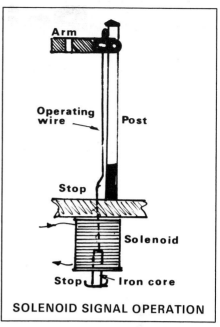

SOLENOID SIGNAL OPERATION

phores are somewhat different. Indeed many people opt out and install dummies. It is better than nothing.

The simplest operation is mechanical, using cord and spring return. However, because signals tend to be installed at the very end, and are often located in awkward places, electrical operation is often favoured.

Because signals are light and do not need locking in place, home made electric signal motors are a practical proposition. A simple signal motor can be built up on a length of tube as shown in the diagram. The number of turns of wire is not critical, the general idea is to fill the bobbins by tumble winding.

A simple way of doing this is to grip a handbrace in a vice, horizontally, with a length of screwed studding in the chuck. The bobbin is threaded on the studding, then secured with a nut.

Enamelled copper wire of around 26 SWG is then wound onto the core. The cheapest sources is an *old* transformer. We stress old, modern transform-

ers have rather better impregnation and all too often the wire cannot be persuaded to unwind.

The armature is cut from a round nail or any other bit of iron wire to hand. The end is drilled to take a length of stiff wire, which is soldered in place. A stop wire is soldered across the bottom to prevent the core going too far up when the current is switched on.

The stiff wire is bent to run alongside the signal post and hooked into the arm. A second stop is wired soldered across the stiff wire as shown at such a point as to leave the arm horizontal. When 12 V DC is applied to the coil the signal is pulled off. A little juggling with the stops is needed to get exactly the right amount of throw into the signal. Fine adjustment is achieved by adjusting the angle of the bends in the operating wire.

If a small relay is to hand, it can be used instead of the home-made solenoid. The relay contacts can be employed for energising a dead section controlled by the signal.

Painting

It is now possible to buy from any well stocked model shop a range of authentic railway colours. Precision Paints offer the biggest selection, Humbrol and Gloy cover the most commonly needed colours in smaller tinlets. In addition, these manufacturers also offer a selection of other colours for use in modelmaking.

Paint is therefore no great problem. Putting it on the model is.

First of all, the model must be clean, which means free from grease. Metal models can be cleaned with almost any cleaner you favour, plastic needs a little more care since a lot of solvents attack it, and therefore warm soapy water is probably best if it has got mucky. A lot of workers take care not to get the plastic parts greasy in the first instance.

With plastic kits it is often a good idea to paint the parts before assembly. This is particularly the case with coach kits, where it is much more convenient to deal with the sides in the flat before glazing.

Metal kits can be improved by beginning with a priming coat. There are various proprietary primers on the market which are excellent for this purpose.

With all paint, the rule is to apply a thin coat, leave to dry and then apply a second. It will take time. Most painting goes wrong because the modeller is in too much of a hurry and tries to apply far too thick a coat.

Spray booth built by the author. A small fan at the rear is wired with the striplight, the compressor is interlocked with the fan. Note paint storage!

Aerosol model paints by Airfix. The range does not, as yet, include railway colours.

Most modellers use tinlets, such as these by Gloy; they are more economical for the quantities needed.

BRUSHES

One of the biggest mistakes anyone can make is to try to paint with indifferent brushes. A good brush today will cost the best part of £1, and therefore needs to be cherished. Always wash it out after use, using the appropriate solvent. In practice, most paints can be cleaned out with relatively inexpensive white spirit.

When this has been done, a final wash in warm soapy water will remove the last of the paint. A proprietary brush cleaner can be used to rectify any small mistakes. Don't allow a brush to harden and never put it in a jar of water in the mistaken idea this will preserve the hairs. The end result is to distort them irreparably.

It is a good idea to store your brushes carefully, making sure their bristles are not under any pressure.

AIRBRUSH

Model painting has been revolutionised by the introduction of the airbrush. This is a sweeping statement, for the airbrush has been around for as long as the hobby has been in existence, but until the last decade airbrushes were only available in specialist artist suppliers and were comparatively expensive. Today most model shops have a simple airbrush in stock, many carry quite advanced equipment.

The elementary airbrush, costing under £10, which works on the principle of the fly spray, by forcing a jet of air across a nozzle, is quite adequate for spraying large areas. There is only minimal control of the jet of paint and therefore masking is an absolute necessity.

The better airbrushes, with needle control, are much better. They range from around £30 upwards, and here the more you pay, the more versatile and accurate the tool.

PROPELLANT OR COMPRESSOR

One reason for the airbrush revolution is the easy availability of aerosol propellant cans, which make it much easier to set up a simple airbrush outfit. However, one can of propellant is just adequate for painting one locomotive, and does not provide enough to allow one to squirt ample air through the brush for cleaning. Since the cans are by no means cheap, it does not take long to discover that some other approach is needed.

Adapter valves are available which screw into a car tyre. If, on a visit to the garage, you blow up the spare tyre to around 60-80 lbs/in², there is enough air to do quite a bit of spraying. Alternatively, one can use a footpump.

However, there is no doubt that, despite its high initial cost, a compressor is the

Set-up for painting a backscene with oil paints in tubes. This is not as difficult as it sounds, providing one remembers that the backscene is only intended to be just that, the detail in the picture is provided by the models themselves.

ideal solution. At the turn of a switch you can get all the compressed air you need and so you can go on spraying for as long as you want. You can even customise the car.

SCOPE OF THE AIRBRUSH

The airbrush is more than just a spraygun in miniature. It is a controllable spray brush, on the better tools while width and density of the spray can be accurately controlled. It is therefore quite easy, given a little practice, to shade one's hues. This is of considerable importance in scenic work, it is also invaluable for weathering locomotives and rolling stock.

However, this is not all. The airbrush enables almost anyone to achieve a smooth, even finish, and yet not lose any fine detail. Furthermore, because a very fine coat is applied, drying is accelerated, and while the normal model colours are not rapid drying, with an airbrush a second coat can be applied some hours after the first, whereas with brush painting, a full 24 hours is advisable.

When two or more colours are to be applied, some form of mask is needed. For very small areas masking can be far too involved and here the use of a good sable brush is advised.

PAINT CONSISTENCY

Model paints are sold mixed for brush application. For spraying they have to be thinned to the consistency of single cream. In general one requires roughly 50% paint to 50% thinners, but as with everything else, experiment is needed to determine the correct balance.

MASKING

For most model railway applications, masking is fairly straightforward. For larger areas, masking tape is best, for two-colour coach liveries, it is virtually obligatory. Unfortunately normal masking tape is too thick and thin self-adhesive tape has too strong a tack. This can be reduced by passing the tape over the corner of a piece of wood before applying it to the coach or wagon.

For more intricate shapes, masking fluid (e.g. Humbrol Maskol) is more convenient. This is a rubbery liquid which dries rapidly. It is applied with an *old* brush over the areas to be masked. When dry the model can be sprayed, then the masking medium can be peeled off.

The use of masking fluid calls for a degree of confidence, since it forms a very lumpy skin and, where successive maskings are called for on a multi-coloured livery the end product appears rather like something out of a horror film. There is, however, a wonderful moment when you strip off the gunge and reveal, in all probability, a beautifully painted model.

When spraying multi-coloured liveries, it is generally a good idea to begin with the lightest colour and then go darker and darker until you reach black.

AEROSOL PAINTS

Many paints are provided in aerosol cans, but at present, no true railway colours are so available.

A number of car colours match railway paints closely. It is difficult to give a list, the manufacturers change the names rather more often than the actual hues! Furthermore, although some people have had success with aerosols, the high cost of paint bought in this fashion means that before long it would be cheaper to get an airbrush which does far more than any aerosol.

SPRAY BOOTH

Any spraygun tends to put paint everywhere else, and although the airbrush is not a serious offender, it is still a good idea to spray in an improvised booth. This need be nothing more than a cardboard carton placed on its side!

One good reason for the spray booth is that because airbrushing puts a good deal of solvent into the air, one is best advised to work outside the home, usually in the garage. The spray booth serves to keep dust off the model whilst spraying.

For serious modelling a permanent spraybooth can be erected in the garage. When spraying anything but water based paints, work in a well ventilated room. There is nothing better ventilated than an empty garage with the doors wide open!

TRANSFERS

One in ten thousand can letter accurately. The majority of us use transfers.

Today it is possible to obtain accurate transfers in most modelling scales for all common British railway insignia. Furthermore, the better makers put these out in sensible packages complete with instructions. Since every type has small variations, it is far better for us to say no more than 'follow the instructions'.

Where commercial transfers fail resort can be made to rub-on lettering, Letraset or Blick. The latter produces a range of

Coal drops and underbridge on a 3mm scale LNER model.

roman and sans serif letters in useful sizes for modellers in a variety of colours, the Letraset range offers more typefaces and is particularly useful for private owner wagons.

However, only a limited selection of Letraset sheets are available other than in black. Given an airbrush, this is no problem. Begin by spraying the wagon (or whatever else you may be lettering) a base colour of the letters. Now apply the Letraset then spray the body colour. Finally detach the Letraset with sticky tape. In effect, you have used the black Letraset as a mask.

IN GENERAL

Painting calls for practice. It is possible that one in 100,000 modellers can do it right first time and then go on to repeat the process, but we have never actually met that lucky individual. Every successful model painter has to learn by practice.

So, we conclude this section with two pieces of advice. First, remember that your first paint job will be far from perfect, but if you persevere, you will achieve competence. Second, it is a good idea to begin with something you intend throwing away.

Garden Railways

Most model railways are situated in an indoor room, which is probably the best arrangement for the smaller scales. However there is one site where there is ample space for the largest of sizes, the garden. Indeed, in the inter-war years, when O gauge was the preferred size, most layouts of any size were situated out of doors.

SCOPE

The garden railway has much to offer, not the least advantage being space. Even the smallest of plots provides ample scope for an interesting system, a normal sized garden allows one to use large sweeping curves, accommodate long trains and still have a considerable distance between stations.

Although it is sometimes believed that OO gauge is 'too small' this is far from the truth. Several highly successful 4 mm scale outdoor systems have been built, but in this scale it is generally accepted that one must arrange storage sidings, if not the principal station, under cover. There is a strong argument for this type of garden railway design, for it permits reasonably

The epitome of the garden railway, Peter Denny's $\frac{3}{8}$in. scale gauge Tamar Valley Light Railway in its original guise.

Raised baseboards in O gauge. The piers are built from concrete blocks, the track is fully ballasted.

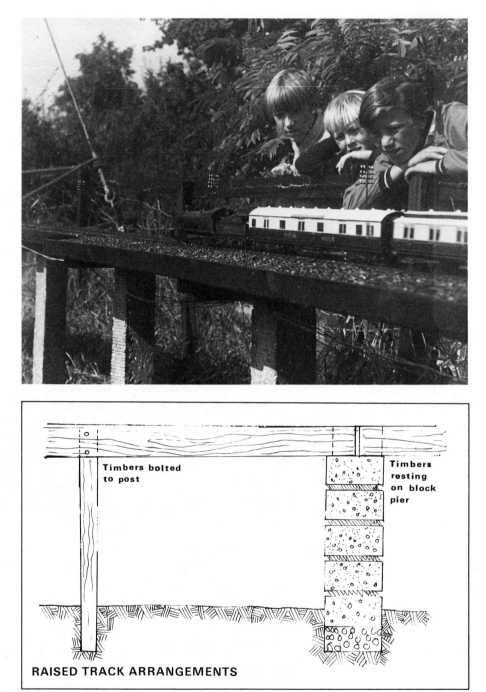

RAISED TRACK ARRANGEMENTS

Timbers bolted to post

Timbers resting on block pier

comfortable operating conditions despite the weather. This particular theme can be carried to extreme, there are several known cases where the entire outdoor section is housed in wooden troughs, protecting the track and rolling stock from the elements, but this is not regarded as a garden railway, but as a railway in a garden.

RAISED CONSTRUCTION

Pre-war outdoor railways were almost invariably carried on timber trestles. We now realise that for many the outbreak of War, which led to their abandonment, neatly avoided the inevitable collapse, for they were carried on the flimsiest of structures. It is now accepted that one must use heavy timber, thoroughly protected against weather. Creosote is still the favoured medium, with used sump oil rapidly growing in favour. Appearance is of secondary importance, since a long trestle structure snaking around the garden tends to look awkward, no matter what.

SUPPORTS

The key to a successful trestle is undoubtedly the support. Whilst timber uprights are easy to use, their propensity to rot in the ground is a serious hazard. Whilst hardwood posts are more resistant, the cost is still high, and in general, concrete is growing in popularity.

The simplest solution is to erect regular piers from concrete blocks or, for a less bleak effect, brick. Here second-hand bricks from a demolition site are ideal, they are relatively cheap and are already weathered. Some garden railway builders have cast their own concrete posts, this is labour intensive and calls for a deal of pre-planning. Whilst concrete fence posts might seem perfect, the basic problem lies in the twin facts of excessive height and the absence of bolt-holes at precisely the right position.

In general, the spacing of supports on a garden railway is far wider than with the normal indoor layout, and so the main timbers are never less than 3 in × ¾ in timber. Some saving is possible if sawn rather than planed timber is bought, for in this setting the rougher finish is of minimal importance.

SURFACES

With the advent of outdoor grade plywood the provision of a durable top surface presents no problems other than cost. It is essential to use at least 12 mm thickness for this purpose. Probably the best material would be second-hand ply shuttering from a building site, if one has the right contacts. Some writers advocate marine ply, this is of course perfect for the purpose, but undoubtedly expensive and, now that most plies employ waterproof adhesives, not absolutely essential. It is, however, essential to specify an outdoor grade.

In the larger scales, plain track can be laid in a ballast trough, or fixed to long sleepers pinned across the longitudinals. These arrangements are not so ideally suited for stations.

SCREENING

The high trestles are gaunt in a garden setting and therefore, unless the garden is large enough for the line to be situated out of direct sight from the house, it is sometimes suggested that shrubs should be planted underneath. This idea, whilst superficially attractive can create problems. For a start, unless the shrubs are kept below the height of the timbers, they will trap moisture and probably hasten rot, whilst their presence will prevent the use of inexpensive timber treatment, and force the employment of the specially formulated preservatives that do not poison plant life.

(Top left) Track on concrete base. (Top right) Track on dwarf walls. (Bottom) Operating pit section.

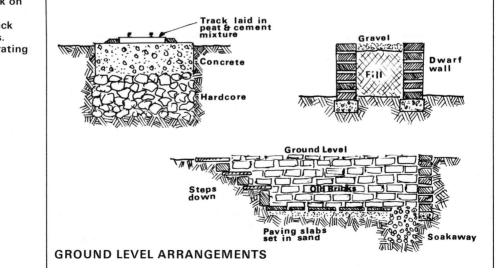

Track laid in peat & cement mixture

Concrete

Hardcore

Gravel

Fill

Dwarf wall

Ground Level

Steps down

Old Bricks

Paving slabs set in sand

Soakaway

GROUND LEVEL ARRANGEMENTS

GROUND LEVEL

This, and the sheer cost of building the trestles, has turned attention towards the ground level line. Here the baseboard, whilst not exactly free (have you priced land lately?) does at least come with the house. However, to lay track directly on dirt, except as a very temporary measure, is to invite trouble.

There are three basic systems. The first is strictly prototypical. A shallow trench is dug along the line of railway, filled with compacted hardcore and the track is laid, in ballast, along the top. At one time the favoured sub-base was ash; in the days when most homes were heated with coal fires, this was not only free, but helped solve the disposal problem.

Today, unless you happen to have a garden laid on stony soil, it usually in-volves purchase. In all cases, the ballast must drain rainwater from the track and provide a degree of grip for the sleepers.

This type of roadbed is liable to frost damage; there is a strong probability that several actions of line will have to be relaid every spring. This movement is not subject to scaling down, and therefore a move-ment which, in full-size practice is a minor annoyance becomes a major cat-astrophe. For this reason there is a grow-ing preference for a concrete sub-base. This can be cast in situ, or take the form of edging slabs bought at the local garden centre. Most workers end up casting in situ, it is not so much that it is cheaper, but that there is a very considerable amount of unalloyed pleasure to be gained from casting concrete in this fashion, for one is not involved in mixing very large quantities, and thus the business of knocking up several hundred-weights is eliminated.

Most authorities favour casting small wooden blocks in the concrete to allow the track to be pinned down. However an alternative is to 'ballast' the track with a cement-peat mixture. This particular mix is not so well known as it should be, the peat is used in place of sand, resulting in a concrete with minimal strength, which can be broken away without undue difficulty. It is, however, reasonably weatherproof and in this particular application gives sufficient strength.

RAISED GROUND LEVEL

Ground level track has one serious disadvantage, backache. There are several answers.

The most obvious is to construct the layout on a dwarf wall or rockery. This is an excellent answer providing you can afford, or find, the quantity of stone required and are prepared for the very considerable amount of work involved.

A less arduous solution is to dig operating pits by the station sites. This reduces the amount of work involved, and

providing the ground is not liable to become waterlogged is a sound solution. The provision of a drainage sump is essential; providing your garden is not on impervious soil, a deep pit full of large stones will suffice.

The ideal solution is where the garden is on undulating land, where it becomes practicable to have the main line on the surface and yet still arrange the stations on raised sections. Indeed, if you are a keen gardener, and have a suitable site, the garden can be terraced to allow both the railway and the plants to show to their best.

PLANTS

Which brings us to the question of keeping a garden railway in tune with the plant life. At first there is a tendency to think in terms of miniature plants, and, undoubtedly, a great deal can be done with this particular aspect of gardening. The only catch is that miniature gardening is, in itself, a very exacting branch of the craft, and is in general carried out on a small scale. To treat completely a modest garden line would be tackling a miniature

One snag with ground level garden railways is that one has to bend down to operate. Apart from that, the arrangement is ideal. This is 16mm scale Festiniog on 32mm gauge track.

16mm scale on O gauge gives 2ft. 0in. narrow gauge ideal for electric or live steam propulsion. Here we have Festiniog stock in action.

garden project of extremely large size.

Fortunately, the overwhelming majority of decorative plants blend happily with small scale models. Agreed, the resulting scene is by no means 'scale' but it is generally agreed that the aesthetic effect is agreeable. In general, the larger annuals are less than happy, small-leaved plants are most suitable. Having said that, the effect of a train curving round a large-leaved specimen shrub is striking and delightful.

There is one important point one must bear in mind, plants grow. Anything near the line is liable to encroach upon the loading gauge and accordingly create difficulties if it is inadvisable to prune. Even where clipping is permissible, one still has to bear in mind the matter of the work involved, not only in cutting the stuff, but in carting it away afterwards.

Oddly enough, grass is the most amenable material. It grows fast, but one can get mechanical devices to deal with this. Lawn mowers are the obvious first thought, but in practice they are unsuitable. The perfect tool is the Black & Decker 'Strimmer' which cuts grass—and anything else with a soft, pithy stem— with a nylon cord whirling at high speed. It will not damage track that is properly laid, though it could harm any very delicate lineside fittings.

TRACK

Track can be made in the conventional fashion on wooden sleepers, a slow and frequently tedious task. Peco Streamline track is, with one important caveat, ideally suited for outdoor use. It is essential to remember that the plastic base does not take kindly to being soaked in most preservatives. Creosote, in particular, is apt to wreak havoc. It does seem, however, that sump oil does not affect the plastic base.

For large scale narrow gauge, Merlin Models have recently introduced a low-cost track based on a pressed metal rail slotted into timber sleepers. It is a little too soon to speak of the durability of this system but with a stainless steel section, and creosoted timbers, it does have a sound pedigree and, being relatively inexpensive, and ready to use it has its attractions.

BRIDGES & VIADUCTS

Bridges and viaducts can be cast in concrete. The main task is the production of the shuttering, the two sides need to be carefully built since any mark on them will be faithfully reproduced in the cast, not once but on every pair of arches.

Reinforcement, in the shape of iron rods has to be introduced before pouring the cement, the other main requirement is, of course, provision for drainage. This is usually achieved by inserting small lengths of tubing in the mould before casting. It does not seem practical to provide cores which, when withdrawn, provide a small weephole.

It is normal to cast the parapet at the same time as the arches are cast. If this is cast onto a pre-formed base it is rather easily broken away from the main mass.

Progress on a viaduct is necessarily slow, each cast has to wait several days to harden. Needless to say, one should only cast concrete during frost-free periods. Furthermore, a cast viaduct is something of a permanency and therefore need to be carefully planned.

Although cast viaducts are normally regarded as a scenic accessory, there is always the possibility, particularly in 4 mm scale garden railways, of constructing the entire sub-structure in this fashion.

All such structures need sound foundations and must not be cast directly onto the ground surface. Settlement of part of the structure will be a serious matter and can lead to the failure of the model.

Girder bridges should be built up from metal or wood. Some degree of simplification of braced structures is permissible.

It is well worthwhile combining a viaduct with an ornamental pond. In such cases, it is worthwhile making provision for draining the pool to permit maintenance. A concrete based pool is preferable, it is asking for trouble to build a viaduct onto a plastic liner.

TUNNELS

Tunnels must conform to two rules. The first is that there should be access in the event of trouble. It is not a good idea to run a length of track through a large drainpipe!

The second is that they should be thoroughly sealed when the line is not in use, otherwise wildlife will take advantage of a ready-made nesting site.

ELECTRIC OPERATION

Normal electric traction can be used out of doors. In the larger scales, O gauge and upward, the use of higher voltages is common, but providing adequate precautions are taken to minimise voltage drop, in particular by providing feeders of adequate cross section and bonding every track joint, 12 V is perfectly successful.

More important is the provision of adequate safeguards when using mains equipment out of doors. It would be well worthwhile installing either an earth leak contact breaker in circuit or interposing a 1:1 isolating transformer in the feed to all outdoor power supplies. Whilst, under normal usage, model railway power units are perfectly safe, the one situation which can lead to risk is their use in wet conditions, when not only can the user be effectively earthed, but, if the casing is soaked, a path could exist between the mains lead and the damp exterior. The two precautions given above, whilst moderately costly, do mean that the loading on the outdoor line is kept within

Station buildings, in Victorian Railway Gothic style, on Peter Denny's garden layout. Solidly constructed and weatherproofed, this model has now survived over 20 years out of doors.

A fine example of garden railway development, the lime works on Peter Denny's Trepolpen Valley Railway, a $\frac{3}{8}$in. scale line in his west-country garden.

safe limits. Better still, keep all mains supplies indoors under cover and take 16 V AC and 12 V DC down to the control points along heavy-duty cable—preferably 1 mm² leads. In this situation normal 'layout wire' is inadequate and will give quite an appreciable voltage drop.

Clockwork drive is obsolescent, not because it is in any way lacking in effectiveness, but because it is no longer manufactured. A common substitute is battery electric. With the increased availability of relatively low consumption high power motors and the advent of small rechargeable cells, the battery powered locomotive is feasible in O gauge and upwards, and not unduly difficult to arrange even in OO gauge. Remote control is another matter, but in the larger scales radio control is growing in favour.

STEAM

Radio control is certainly coming in as a means of taming live steam. This particular approach is growing in popularity in both Gauge 1, and in the very popular

16 mm scale narrow gauge, which uses 32 mm (O gauge) track and represents 2 ft gauge prototype practice. (With $\frac{3}{8}$in scale 32 mm is virtually metre gauge). Live steam is ideal for garden use, where there are no arguments about the smell and mess and the only things you can possibly set alight are the sleepers.

HAZARDS

Wildlife is a permanent hazard. Tunnels will be used as nesting sites, whilst a variety of animals will use the tracks either as walkways, or for sunning themselves. In the larger scales, George Stephenson's classic comment comes to mind, it is usually a case of 'the waur for the coo—or cat or whatever.' In most cases there is little damage, cats in particular seem very quick to know when trains are running and depart with haste and dignity.

A more serious hazard of comparatively recent growth is vandalism. For this reason it is even more than ever essential to ensure that the railway is not visible to the casual passer by.

The Next Stages

In this book I have concentrated on those aspects of a model railway which cannot be found in brightly coloured boxes on the dealer's shelves, those parts which have to be tackled by the enthusiast himself—or herself, as the case may be. Obviously there is more, in point of fact, a great deal more. There is the temptation to imply that the reader should move on, to specialise, to become more expert.

Why?

The creation of a complete model railway which looks realistic and works reliably is no mean task in itself. Anyone who does so need not feel he, or she, is somehow lacking if this is where the matter rests. That a small minority in the hobby have moved further, often by specialising in some aspect of the hobby, does not mean that everyone should follow. But, if there remains a feeling that something more could be achieved, then there are some well explored paths to follow.

The first I would suggest does not involve actual construction. On a well designed model railway, it is possible to operate the trains exactly in accordance with full sized practice, with a full working timetable and, frequently, the refinement of traffic circulars amending the time-table. In addition, there is the business, not only of devising authentic train formations but additionally, arranging locomotive rosters and finally, the offering of traffic for the freight side.

Scratchbuilding rampant! A corner of Mike Sharman's early Victorian railway workshop scene, with mixed gauge turntable. The locomotive being turned is one of his favourite types, a Crampton single wheeler.

The Model Railway Club's 2 mm scale 'Chiltern Green' is one of the most widely acclaimed models to appear on the exhibition circuit in recent years. The reason is not difficult to find, it is a model based loosely on part of the former Midland main line, and includes an accurate model of the distinctive viaduct just south of Chiltern Green itself. The landscape has been slightly compressed and subtly altered to enhance the effect.

This can be done as easily with coaches, wagons and locomotives straight out of the box as it can with individually scratchbuilt items. Indeed, if anything, it is more common with r-t-r stock because, if a great deal of one's time is taken up building models then there is that much less for working the railway.

At its more advanced levels, model railway operation tends to get a trifle exacting, though, to the confirmed operator, this is all part of the fun. A great deal is undoubtedly a matter of being a real railwayman in miniature, of running services to provide for an imaginary community in a logical, realistic manner. However, when it comes to throwing dice to determine loadings, let alone, as I have encountered, employing a computer to generate random factors it could be considered to be going a little too far. Though, there is the point that, if something does go wrong, a properly programmed computer could announce that the small scale NUR or ASLEF have gone on strike! It isn't, of course, necessary to go quite as far as this, but even an elementary schedule of operations is far better than aimless running; that is nothing more nor less than playing trains!

Whilst scratchbuilding, the creation of a model from raw materials and a few basic components is still held to be the ultimate end of modelling in many quarters, the construction of a kit, or the skilful modification of a ready built model is something of a craft in its own right. Certainly, to get the very best from a good kit, one needs to use a good deal of care, and at rock bottom, the distinction between this and skill is hard to define. As for modifying a ready-to-run model, where this is done so that the alterations are indistinguishable, the skill and artistry involved are considerable. For my part, I consider scratchbuilding the easier option, at least, you are not involved in taking things apart!

The question of painting, repainting, correct lining and lettering, and weathering is one where the care and skill of the individual pays considerable dividends. This is one area where practice is essential, despite many assertions, there are no wonder methods that guarantee results.

Electrification is a field where, more than any other, the individual can let himself rip. The plain fact of the matter is that although the majority of model railways can be effectively worked by

A model timber yard. The elaborate gantry is a Mikes Models kit.

The end of the line, a model of a disused branch disappearing into a bricked-up tunnel. Some modellers licence is present, it is more than likely that the signal and track would have been removed.

extremely simple methods, anyone who has grasped the basic principles of electrification and who enjoys wiring for its own sake can produce as high a degree of complexity as he likes. The simplest of layouts can have a full-fledged centralised control panel, replete with lights, that will excite the viewer. That the information it provides could as readily be obtained by glancing at the model, that the impressive switchgear does little more than a simpler panel could perform is totally irrelevant, one indulges in such ploys for their own sake. In extreme cases, the railway only exists to justify the wiring, and to give some point to the circuitry.

I have left to last what can be the most dangerous specialisation of all, the scenic and architectural field. Its perils lie in its very virutes.

First of all, despite the existence of stereotyped housing estates, buildings vary enormously, and since, even in 2 mm scale there is little room for more than a few true to scale structures, the architectural modeller selects the more interesting facades. It is an area where scratchbuilding pays the best dividends, because this infinite variety can only be achieved by considering each building as a unique model project. Furthermore, even the most costly of materials in this field are relatively inexpensive. Finally, there is nothing quite so attractive to the eye as a pleasing model scene which looks absolutely authentic. So, in all directions, it pays dividends.

The danger lies in the fact that the railway tends to take a back seat. The first great exponent of this craft, John H. Ahern, whose Madder Valley can be seen at Pendon Museum, succeeded in keeping the railway to the fore. Others have been less successful, usually by accident. The present past master of the craft, Dave Rowe, is unabashed, in his dioramas, the railway content is minimal.

How does one develop? One piece of advice is to join the local club. Certainly, quite a few people have benefitted in this fashion, but there are qualifications. The first is that there must be a local club, and then this club must be in good heart. I have known clubs where the overall level of modelling is low to middling, and where everyone is happy to muddle along in a slap-happy fashion. There is nothing wrong with this, the members like it that way, and are free to do so, but it won't help anyone raise his standards.

Then it is essential that you are free to attend meetings. Merely paying a subscription provides no benefit to you. So, it helps if the club meet regularly at a time and place convenient to you otherwise there isn't a lot you will gain from membership.

Finally, there are, of course, the model magazines. They are all good, though not necessarily to your particular taste, at least, in any one issue chosen at random. To get the full flavour of a magazine you need to see three recent issues. I stress recent, since all journals evolve, and the fact that one was good in the 1960's doesn't make it good in the 1980's. However, I venture to suggest that, if you have enjoyed this book, then you will find that Model Railways, the magazine I edit, is very much to your taste.